Praise for *The Financial Times Guide to Foreign Exchange Trading*

'The must-read Bible for everything there is to know about the forex markets and trading. Miss it at your own peril.'

Lianna Brinded, Journalist and Broadcaster

'Stuart gives a comprehensive introduction to the inner workings of the currency markets, outlining how all the different elements link together, at the same time warning of the perils and pitfalls to the unwary.

He underlines the importance of effective risk management using the time honoured tools of technical analysis in any effective trading strategy.'

Michael Hewson, Senior Market Analyst (CFTe), CMC Markets UK

The Financial Times Guide to Foreign Exchange Trading

PEARSON

At Pearson, we believe in learning – all kinds of learning for all kinds of people. Whether it's at home, in the classroom or in the workplace, learning is the key to improving our life chances.

That's why we're working with leading authors to bring you the latest thinking and the best practices, so you can get better at the things that are important to you. You can learn on the page or on the move, and with content that's always crafted to help you understand quickly and apply what you've learned.

If you want to upgrade your personal skills or accelerate your career, become a more effective leader or more powerful communicator, discover new opportunities or simply find more inspiration, we can help you make progress in your work and life.

Pearson is the world's leading learning company. Our portfolio includes the Financial Times, Penguin, Dorling Kindersley, and our educational business, Pearson International.

Every day our work helps learning flourish, and wherever learning flourishes, so do people.

To learn more please visit us at: www.pearson.com/uk

The Financial Times Guide to Foreign Exchange Trading

Stuart Fieldhouse

Harlow, England • London • New York • Boston • San Francisco • Toronto • Sydney • Auckland • Singapore • Hong Kong
Tokyo • Seoul • Taipei • New Delhi • Cape Town • São Paulo • Mexico City • Madrid • Amsterdam • Munich • Paris • Milan

Pearson Education Limited

Edinburgh Gate
Harlow CM20 2JE
Tel: +44 (0)1279 623623
Website: www.pearson.com/uk

First published 2012

© Pearson Education Limited 2012 (print and electronic)

The right of Stuart Fieldhouse to be identified as author of this work has been asserted by him in accordance with the Copyright, Designs and Patents Act 1988.

Pearson Education is not responsible for the content of third-party internet sites.

ISBN: 978-0-273-75183-0 (print)
    978-0-273-75184-7 (PDF)
    978-0-273-75185-4 (ePub)

British Library Cataloguing-in-Publication Data
A catalogue record for the print edition is available from the British Library

Library of Congress Cataloging-in-Publication Data
A catalog record for the print edition is available from the Library of Congress

The *Financial Times*. With a worldwide network of highly respected journalists, The *Financial Times* provides global business news, insightful opinion and expert analysis of business, finance and politics. With over 500 journalists reporting from 50 countries worldwide, our in-depth coverage of international news is objectively reported and analysed from an independent, global perspective. To find out more, visit www.ft.com/pearsonoffer.

10 9 8 7 6 5 4 3 2 1
16 15 14 13 12

Typeset in 9/13pt ITC Stone Serif Std by 3
Print edition printed and bound in Great Britain by Ashford Colour Press Ltd, Gosport

NOTE THAT ANY PAGE CROSS REFERENCES REFER TO THE PRINT EDITION

To my parents. For believing.

Contents

About the author

Stuart Fieldhouse is an experienced financial journalist. He spent many years at the FT Group including two years as editor of *International Wealth Management* (FT Business), was co-editor of the *FT Fraud Report*, and was founder editor of *Institutional Alternative Investment* and *The Hedge Fund Journal*.

He has worked with the product development team at CMC Markets, one of the leading financial spread betting companies. In this role he worked on the dealing floor, as well as with the global head of trading, matching new markets to spread betting products. He was part of the design team that developed CMC's brand new spread betting platform, launched in the UK in 2010.

He has also worked very closely with hedge funds over the years, including as part of the marketing team of a major $15 billion fund-linked structured products business, and has advised one of the leading currency-based hedge fund businesses in Europe on its corporate communications.

Acknowledgements

Author's Acknowledgements

Several individuals played a key role in bringing this book into being. In particular, I'd like to thank Ashraf Laidi at City Index for his many, many conversations with me on the topic of forex and monetary policy when we were both at CMC Markets. At Accendo Markets I'd like to thank Michael van Dulken for his help with the technical analysis chapter. Others who played a role in aiding my research for the book include Michael Hewson at CMC Markets, Mariya Rysin, Michael Morton at The Armchair Trader, Marcus Panton, Rupert Vaughan Williams, Cindy Heidebluth at Alpari, Renaud Cohard and Bill McIntosh at *The Hedge Fund Journal*, the guys at IKOS, Martin Lykke at NPforex and, as ever, Vanya Dragomanovich for her outstanding analysis on interest rates, political risk and precious metals markets.

Publisher's Acknowledgements

We are grateful to the following for permission to reproduce copyright material:

Figures

Figure 3.7 from www.livecharts.co.uk, LiveCharts.co.uk; Figures 5.1 and 5.2 from www.alphaterminal.co.uk, Alpha Terminal screen shots reproduced by kind permission of Ionic Information Ltd; Figures 6.1, 6.2, 6.4, 8.7, 8.8 and 8.9 from www.babypips.com; Figure 6.3 reprinted with permission from Yahoo! Inc. 2012 Yahoo! Inc. YAHOO! and the YAHOO! logo are trademarks of Yahoo! Inc.; Figure 6.5 and table in appendix from The Armchair Trader, www. thearmchairtrader.com; Figure 8.2 from Alpari, www.alpari.co.uk; Figure 8.6 from www.aboutcurrency.com.

Tables

Table 6.1 from www.sucdenfinancial.com.

In some instances we have been unable to trace the owners of copyright material, and we would appreciate any information that would enable us to do so.

1

Foreign exchange trading: getting started

Foreign exchange trading represents one of the fastest-growing areas of retail investment finance in the world today. In the last few years in particular, the number of people who own a foreign exchange dealing account has mushroomed. Interest in currencies is running at an all-time high.

The very fact that you are reading this sentence means there is something about the currency markets that has captured your interest. You may be intrigued about the idea of working full-time as a trader, or you may be seeking a new investment opportunity that is not correlated to stock or bond markets. With the prevailing crisis in the Eurozone, currencies and their impact on global economies have become a major issue for governments, central banks and the financial world in general. As they have come to dominate the headlines, so too has interest in trading these volatile markets increased.

But what is foreign exchange trading all about really? How does it work, and how can you, as a private individual, profit from this market? This book sets out to act as a primer for the newcomer to foreign exchange – or FX – trading. It will give you a solid grounding in the currency markets, what makes them move, and how to trade them. It includes information on choosing a brokerage to deal through, and how to manage many of the common risks that trading can present you with. It can also help with fitting currencies into a larger investment strategy, be it other futures markets or a physical portfolio.

Trading foreign exchange can be approached in a number of ways – there is no 'right' way to trade FX. Many individuals have become wealthy following radically different strategies, and some have combined good fortune and discipline in the course of their trading careers to be able to retire early. In this book, we examine some of the more common approaches used to trade FX markets. Finally, we also look at some of the useful resources that traders can use to improve their performance.

What do we mean by foreign exchange trading?

Foreign exchange traders deal in currencies. Like individuals who buy a foreign currency when they go on holiday, FX traders are buying and selling the currencies issued by various countries. But unlike your average holidaymaker, FX traders are doing this for profit, trying to make money from the changing relative values between the various freely traded currencies around the world.

Currencies are typically traded as 'pairs': this means you are buying one currency and selling another. When you go on holiday, you are selling your base currency (the currency you get paid in) and buying that of the country you are going to visit. For example, you might be selling British pounds to a currency exchange and buying euros. Currency traders don't just buy and sell their home currency, however. They might trade the euro against the Japanese yen, or the Australian dollar against the South Korean won. What their base currency may be is not necessarily relevant. Just because you get paid in US dollars does not mean that you can only trade the USD against other currencies.

The global forex markets are a little different from some other financial markets, such as shares or commodities. For starters, there is no widely recognised exchange on which currencies are traded. Instead, prices are set by the interbank market – large banks and other participants who are big-volume buyers and sellers deal currencies between themselves, not on a currency exchange. The prices they determine in their trading are passed onto the brokers, who in turn quote them to traders.

One of the advantages of this is that there is no point at which global forex markets are really closed, although sometimes it can be difficult to find someone to quote you a price on a Sunday. Most of the time, however, someone, somewhere, always seems to be trading forex. This means that increasingly brokers are able to quote prices around the clock, and individual traders are able to execute trades around the clock. It makes it possible for investors to trade FX when they get home from work, or in the middle of the night. In addition, there is less risk of prices gapping as a consequence of overnight news: stock markets can be subject to sudden moves as soon as trading opens in the morning, sudden jumps or falls which can catch traders out. Currency markets, because of their 24-hour nature, are less subject to sudden gaps caused by market closure.

Another big advantage of currency markets is the fact that they are highly liquid. Liquidity is a measure of how easy it is to buy or sell something – an illiquid investment, like a house for example, can take a very long time to sell. Forex, however, is one of the easiest and fastest markets to get in and out of. This is because the large daily volumes traded in global currencies – far outstripping other traditional financial markets – mean more competitive pricing and narrower spreads, particularly in the major currencies.

According to Bloomberg, a premier site for business and financial market news, the daily volume in US Treasuries (US government debt) is about $300 billion and on the New York Stock Exchange $25 billion in shares changes hands on a daily basis. By contrast, the average daily volume in global currency markets in 2010 was $4 trillion. This gives you some idea of how currency markets dwarf other financial markets in terms of their daily liquidity. It also means it is easy to place trades in the market at the price you are quoted, and get out of the market quickly if you want to. In short, many of the inconveniences that come with other markets – for example, paying a bank or brokerage a fee to hold your electronic stock certificates – can be eliminated in currency trading. It is this level of efficiency that is proving to be one of the big selling points for foreign exchange as an asset class for individual investors.

Currencies are always quoted in pairs in the international forex markets (see Table 1.1). You will never see a currency quoted in isolation – it has to be measured against something else, usually another currency. Most frequently, this will be the US dollar, still the de facto reserve currency of the world, but other non-dollar currency pairs are also frequently traded.

Table 1.1 Most traded currency pairs (average daily volume April 2011)

EUR/USD	31%	$245.1bn
USD/JPY	12%	$96.8bn
USD/CAD	10%	$76.9bn
GBP/USD	8%	$66.1bn
USD/BRL	2%	$17.9bn
USD vs other currencies	24%	$194bn
EUR vs other currencies	7%	$54.4bn
All other currency pairs	6%	$47.3bn

Source: Federal Reserve Bank of New York

Each currency is also assigned a three-letter code. Table 1.2 shows some of the more common ones.

Table 1.2 Commonly traded currencies and their codes

Currency	*Code*
US dollar	USD
Euro	EUR
Japanese yen	JPY
British pound	GBP
Swiss franc	CHF
Australian dollar	AUD
Canadian dollar	CAD
New Zealand dollar	NZD
Singapore dollar	SGD
Hong Kong dollar	HKD

Each currency pair will be quoted as a pair, for example:

GBP/USD   1.6035/1.6037

What you're looking at here is the amount in the currency on the right of the slash mark – in this case the US dollar – that you can use to buy one unit of the currency on the left – the British pound (GBP). The numbers always refer to the currency on the right, the so-called quote currency.

But why are there two figures? As with a currency exchange at an airport, there is one price at which you can buy this currency pair and one at which you can sell it. The difference is known as the spread. This is how the currency brokerages make their money.

Let's have a look at another often traded currency pair:

USD/JPY   77.985/77.987

Here we have the US dollar being traded against the Japanese yen. In this case you can buy almost 78 yen for your American dollar.

Of pips and ticks

Currency traders will tend to focus on the figure on the far right of the quote, as this is the number that will be changing most frequently during an average day's trading. Because currencies usually change only marginally, money is made on the tiny, fractional moves in relative prices. In the USD/JPY example given above, this is 0.001 of a yen. This is commonly called a 'pip'.

Ticks are the minimum price increment quoted by a broker. A tick can also be the same thing as a pip, but not always. In the case of the yen, one broker might quote you a tick size of 0.001 as above, but another might quote 0.0010. You should be able to tell from the trading screen you are using, but if you're not sure, ask your account provider.

Tick sizes can also vary depending on the type of account you are using to trade currencies with. As a rule of thumb, most brokers quote out to five decimal places in most of the big currency pairs – for example, you might see EUR/USD quoted at 1.27236. This can often be a further decimal place than you would see at a typical cash foreign exchange shop.

With the yen example above, because the numbers to the left of the decimal place can often fluctuate as well, brokers will tend not to quote the JPY out to more than three decimal places.

Do I need to be a financial professional to trade forex successfully?

From the outset, this book assumes that you are *not* a financial professional, that you do not work in the City of London, and that you may not even have traded other financial markets such as shares or commodities before. Indeed, there is no real need to have had experience of trading financial markets in order to open a forex trading account and get started. The FX markets are not reserved for City traders who want to continue to trade after hours: most of the professional traders I've met would rather do anything but with their spare time.

What has impressed me about foreign exchange is the sheer diversity of the individuals who trade it: people from all walks of life and backgrounds are already active FX traders. I have met retired traders, and traders who are university students in their early twenties. More than one housewife is supplementing her monthly income by trading in between school drop-off and pick-up. Others get home from work and trade currency markets rather than watch television. For some it is a hobby, for others a lifestyle. With the introduction of mobile technology, it is now possible to trade wherever you can find an internet connection. Whether it is a good thing to be almost continually connected to the markets is debatable, but the opportunity is now there for those who want it.

It is important, however, that you understand the risks involved in FX trading, that you know exactly what it is you are trading, and that you also have a fair idea of what the company providing you with your account is allowed to do and what it is not allowed to do. There is no point complaining if the firm you trade with is acting within the limits of the regulations laid down by its local regulator.

This book can help you with finding and opening an account with an FX broker, and tells you about the different types of FX trading accounts that are available to the private investor. Not all types of trading account are available in every country, and there are a number of different types of products you can use to trade forex, some more expensive than others.

This book also examines the major and minor currencies that are available to trade and what sets them apart. The good thing about forex is that you have far fewer markets to follow.

Unlike the thousands of shares you can trade in the equities markets, most forex traders restrict themselves to less than 20 currency pairs. You can have the charts for most of the major currency pairs up on a single computer screen.

I also cover off some of the major economic announcements and other possible factors that can affect forex markets, and look at some recent examples of this in action. This is called 'trading the news' and is an approach favoured by some traders and not by others. Still, it helps for all traders to have some degree of knowledge about what factors move currency markets.

There is also a chapter on risk management, including how to avoid losing all your trading capital early on. This is arguably one of the most important chapters in this book, since it is possible for even a more experienced trader to blunder into trading margined forex and quickly lose a substantial sum of money. There are many tales of novice traders who enter these markets only to lose most or all of their trading money in their first few weeks or months, when following a few simple risk-management procedures could save them a great deal of heartache.

There is no right or wrong way to trade foreign currency and much of your success in this respect will be down to finding a system that suits you, both as an individual and in terms of the lifestyle that you lead.

This book can provide you with information on some of the favoured strategies employed by FX traders. Of all the financial markets, forex is in many ways the 'purest' in that it is so efficient – apart from the intervention by central banks, it is very hard for a single bank, fund manager or other investor to consistently influence the course of the market. FX is thus a favoured market for those traders who like to develop systematic, rules-based trading strategies, or who have written computer programs to provide them with buy and sell signals in a given currency market. If this sounds of interest, this book will be able to point you in the right direction.

We will also look at some of the additional resources out there for traders, including FX-specific resources, and in the appendix I provide a table showing some of the top forex brokerages and what sorts of services they offer. Hopefully this will provide a starting point for you, the reader, to carry out more specialised research and reading in the areas of forex trading that particularly interest you.

Finding a forex broker

Many experienced currency traders have more than one trading account. There are a number of good reasons for multiple accounts, and if you can afford it, it can be worth doing. FX trading companies come in all shapes and sizes. Most will offer the same core range of currency markets, but beyond that there are many ways to differentiate them. Before opening an account, it is worth shopping around using the criteria that are important for you.

Access to FX trading facilities will largely depend on where you live. Foreign exchange trading is a global pastime, and you will find traders in all the many far-flung corners of the world. Today, the most popular way to invest in forex is by using contracts for difference (CFDs). These are essentially over-the-counter (OTC) derivatives that you can trade using a broker as your counterparty. They let you get access to currency movements while taking advantage of margin facilities: in effect, borrowing money from a broker to trade with, but keeping the profits.

CFDs are easy to trade online, and there are now several major global brokerages offering CFD accounts to trade forex with. CFDs can also be used to trade other markets, such as stock markets, bonds, shares in companies and commodities. It is just important to remember that these are derivative contracts – that means you are not buying or selling the actual, physical underlying asset, you are just trying to make money from changes in price.

The market for CFDs is becoming increasingly competitive as more firms set up shop and more banks seek to offer their clients CFD trading facilities. This is good news for you, the retail trader, because it means you are able to shop around for the best trading account for your purposes. Judge firms by the criteria that are important to you as a trader: do not open an account simply because there is a special offer on, or a company is offering you $250 of its own money to open an account.

The intense competition is, however, helping to narrow the spreads investors are offered by forex brokerages. A spread is the distance between the price you can buy at and the price you can sell at. The spread, more than anything else, is how brokers make their money. From your perspective as a budding trader, the spread is an indication of how expensive it is to trade a particular market.

In the UK and the Republic of Ireland, an alternative to CFDs is the financial spread betting account. This is the favoured FX trading format for residents in those countries, as it is treated as gambling for tax purposes and is therefore tax free. Unlike CFDs traded in the UK, spread betting is not subject to capital gains tax or stamp duty.

Beyond CFDs and spread betting, however, there are other ways to trade FX markets. In the US, neither spread betting nor CFDs are available. Traders instead tend to use margined FX accounts where they are borrowing money to buy and sell currency in the actual forex market, or they trade exchange-cleared foreign exchange futures. There are other ways to profit from forex price movements as well, which I explore in more detail later in this book.

Can forex brokers be trusted?

FX trading companies are highly profitable entities. They make their money primarily on the spreads they offer on currency markets, but they also profit in other ways. Unlike investing in funds or physical shares, some of the costs associated with currency trading are not immediately obvious and will differ from company to company. When trading it is useful to be aware of how your FX broker – your counterparty – is making money as well. Many complaints from new traders originate because they feel they are somehow being 'tricked' or 'short changed' by a firm. Often this boils down to the terms and conditions of the account that has been opened, or the specific trading instrument that is being used.

Some firms may actually offer you money to open an account with them, usually an amount that is credited to your account.   Where's the catch there? It is often entrenched in the terms and conditions. Apply a degree of scepticism to everything you are offered by trading companies. Ultimately, trading boils down to the price your currency trade is executed at; everything else is just window dressing.

Once you have a firm you are happy using, I'd suggest you stick with them, and then open a second account to allow objective analysis of the service you are getting from your first trading shop. This is especially the case with prices and execution. Although you may see a price quoted for a particular currency pair, this will not necessarily be the price you see on your trading screen, or the price you will be able to execute at. But why?

FX trading companies often act as a form of market maker. They 'make' a price on a financial market for you to trade. They are starting to provide some traders with what is called direct market access (DMA), but in reality there are two entities which sit between you, the trader, and the global currency markets. Although the interbank market may publish an official price, and you may see this duplicated elsewhere, for example on a Bloomberg terminal, it is not the price you will trade on.

Between the currency markets and the FX company sits another beast, usually an investment bank acting as a prime broker. A retail trading brokerage may use several prime brokers to give it access to currency markets in order to find the best price for its customers. Some prime brokers are retained because they specialise in a particular market and can procure the best price there is. The FX company is looking at the various prices being quoted to it by the prime brokers and will then pick a price at which it feels confident it can execute the trade that it can also quote back to its customers.

The price you trade at is the price your broker quotes to you, not the price you might see from another source. It is important to realise early on that there is no use complaining to your broker that they are consistently quoting USD/JPY a number of pips away from what you can see on Bloomberg, because you can't *trade* on the price you see on Bloomberg. The most effective way to compare prices is to have two trading accounts with different providers and see who is quoting you a consistently more accurate price. This is one of the reasons experienced traders in the FX markets make use of more than one account.

The solution to all this is to trade via a DMA account, which lets you trade actual forex rather than CFDs or spread bets, which are generally classed as OTC derivatives.

Also be sure that the broker you choose is properly regulated. Look into what the investor compensation arrangements are if the broker you trade with should go to the wall, because it does happen. The situation is becoming more complicated as a broker in one country might be servicing client accounts in dozens of others. Forex is becoming an increasingly global industry, and unravelling the failure of a brokerage an increasingly complex task for accountants and regulators. And just because the parent broker you deal with is sitting in a tightly regulated jurisdiction like Switzerland or the UK does not mean that the subsidiary you deal with is similarly regulated. Always check.

Other differentiating factors

Here are some other differentiating factors between brokerages to consider before you write that cheque. You can also refer to the back of this book for a quick comparison of some of the major players.

Minimum account size: some brokers will require a minimum amount of money is held in your account before you can trade.

Demo accounts: these are 'paper' trading accounts which let you trade with play money. Some firms let you use these to try out their trading platforms. Most will still restrict you to a couple of weeks before they shut you off (unless you open a live account with real money, of course).

Mobile trading: this is becoming increasingly prevalent, but not all brokers offer mobile trading across all mobile platforms. It is now possible to trade forex with both mobile phones and tablets and the interfaces on offer are becoming increasingly sophisticated.

Seminars and training: some brokers offer both live and web-based training and education, most of which is free. These can be particularly useful when you are starting out. More advanced trader training can be obtained from a variety of sources.

Trading platforms: many FX brokerages will offer their own proprietary trading platforms, while others will require you to purchase and set up your own software, which can be expensive. Not all trading platforms are created equal either: some are proprietary, having been developed at great expense by some leading brokers, while others are off-the-shelf applications. They can be downloaded onto a PC or used via the web.

Expert advisers: EAs are trading programs that can inform you about when to buy or sell. They tend to be more disciplined than human traders and can be particularly helpful if you are still unsure of yourself or making consistent mistakes. They do come with strings attached, however, usually higher fees or higher minimum account size.

2

Accessing the markets: different types of FX trading account

There is a broad range of FX trading accounts available. Much will depend on where in the world you live. These days, CFDs have come to dominate much of the online retail FX trading market, with spread betting still the most popular format in the UK. However, traders based in North America will not have access to either of these.

There are now many different trading platforms out there, some better than others, and most spread betting companies have spent a lot of money in the development of their own proprietary trading platforms.

As discussed in the previous chapter, you will find currency trades will be quoted using two prices, not one. This is called the bid/offer spread and is the same as buying or selling foreign currency across the counter at a bank or post office. There is one price to buy at, and one price to sell at, and the buy price is always higher than the sell price. The difference in the prices is called the spread.

Spreads continue to be a major source of competition between the various FX brokers, as they seek to attract customers by offering narrower and narrower spreads (and effectively cheaper trading). You will frequently see the most popular currency markets will have very small spreads, with only a few points difference. The hope, of course, is that traders will be tempted to trade other markets as well, where the spread is a lot wider. Emerging markets currencies will tend to have wider spreads.

Each currency market will also have a margin rate, as described previously. This represents the amount of money you will need to post up front when you open the trade. It will vary from 1 per cent, all the way up to 50 per cent in some extreme cases. Margins for currency trades tend to be uniformly low because currency markets are so liquid and it is easy for brokers to hedge their positions as a result.

Margin rates can change quickly during periods of crisis in the global financial system – for example, during the credit crunch in 2008 – and then even margins on currency trades can jump to 50 per cent or even higher. Brokers are within their rights to turn round and require a 100 per cent margin is posted immediately or they will close your trades.

Be aware, however, that the broker is still lending you money to margin trade and will charge you interest on that, usually in the form of an overnight financing charge. This is a very real cost of margin trading, and you will need to factor that into your overall costs. In addition, brokers will charge commissions on trades and these will vary from firm to firm. It is worth doing some homework on the active brokers to see what their total charges add up to.

Spread betting

Financial spread betting is currently the most popular way to trade FX markets in the UK and Ireland. This is primarily because it is tax free, as it is considered gambling for tax purposes by Her Majesty's Revenue and Customs Service. Those who use a spread betting account have to be resident in either the UK or the Republic of Ireland. These accounts will not be made available to you outside these jurisdictions. Spread bets are free of capital gains tax or any stamp duty, allowing you to pocket your winnings without paying tax. The downside is that you cannot use your losses to claim back tax either.

With spread betting, trading currencies involves staking an amount of money per point the price moves. A typical example would be £1/ point on the GBP/USD, where each point is effectively a single tick. If the currency pair goes up, you're making money to the tune of how many points it has risen.

Profits – and losses – in spread betting are measured in points. The more money you attach to each point, the bigger your risk and the larger your potential profits or losses. If GBP/USD closed up 25 pips today, and my bet was staked at £1 per point, I'd make £25 (minus the spread, of course). If I instead staked £3 per pip, I'd make £75.

Once you decide to sell your position, you hit the sell button and you've closed your trade. If you've made a profit, you've done it tax free, as spread betting profits are not taxed in the UK.

Contracts for difference (CFDs)

Contracts for difference, more commonly called CFDs, are the most popular global instrument for trading foreign exchange. Unless you are living in the United States or Canada, you should be able to access a CFD trading account. There are a number of major global CFD providers that are equipped to take on clients from most countries, and some offshore specialists that are specifically marketing to residents outside the main CFD markets.

CFD trading is particularly popular in countries like Australia and Germany, but there are active CFD traders in more than 100 countries around the world. Unlike spread bets, CFDs trading in the UK or Ireland is not treated as gambling and hence is not tax free. This means you will have to pay UK (or Irish) capital gains tax (CGT) on any profits if you live in those countries. It also means you may be able to offset losses sustained in your CFD account against CGT in other areas.

It is worth consulting an accountant, as the range of tax credits available in this area is large and complex. CFDs may also be subject to tax in other countries.

CFDs are not traded using the price per point system that spread bets use. Instead, a CFD will have a price at which you will buy it and a price at which you will sell it (with the usual bid/offer spread, of course). Your profit is simply the difference in price. In many ways, it is more like buying and selling shares than spread betting.

Example

CFD trade

Here is an example of a CFD trade using the popular currency pair of EUR/USD:

A CFD pays out to you based on the change in the price at which you bought the CFD and which you sold it.

Let's say you buy a CFD for EUR/USD at 1.27961 (bid) and 1.27968 (offer). There is a spread of seven pips on this contract.

Deciding that the currency is going to appreciate, we use the offer price (1.27968). The pair is quoted at 1 per cent margin. We decide to commit $100, giving us $10,000 worth of CFD.

Remember: if trading forex with CFDs you are not buying or selling actual currency, you are simply gambling on the change in the price.

Let's say the euro increases in value and the price of the CFD goes to 1.30018. This represents a change of 2050 pips. However, if the spread is still seven points, we'll need to use the bid price to exit the trade, at 1.30011. Still, that's 2043 pips. But how much did we make?

If the USD is the 'quote' currency (the currency on the right), you can use the following formula:

Profit = (price change in pips) × (units traded)

In this case, we are calculating your total risk in the market, not the money you put down as margin, so it is a $10,000 trade initially, *not* $100.

Profit = 0.02043 × 10,000 = $204.30

What I have not figured into this are commissions and financing charges that would be levied by your broker. This will differ from broker to broker and will also depend on how long you keep your trade open.

However, let's say your base account is in USD and you're trading GBP/EUR. You're still focusing on the change in the number of pips, remember. With $100, you might see a buy quote for GBP/EUR at 1.21043. You think that the euro is going to weaken against the pound. Although the euro is now your quote currency and the dollar is not involved, you are still trading the price change in dollars. Once again, with CFDs you are not trading real currency, just changes in price.

Using the bid price, you are effectively shorting the GBP and expecting it to be worth fewer euros at the end of the day.

The price falls by 1000 pips to 1.20043 (for simplicity's sake). Let's assume the same seven-point spread and 1 per cent margin (for a total price change of 993 pips).

Profit = 0.00993 × 10,000 = $99.30

CFDs were originally dreamed up in the investment banking industry, and are still popular with institutional investors such as hedge funds and private banks. In other respects, CFDs can be very similar to spread bets.

Margined foreign exchange

This type of account is the most popular way to trade FX in the US, and is also readily available in many other countries, although it is beginning to lose ground to CFD trading internationally. The big difference between margined FX trading and CFDs is that the broker is providing you with direct exposure to the FX market. Unlike CFDs and spread betting (above), the prices on your trading screen should more accurately reflect the prices in the interbank market. As a result, those traders using more of an automated approach to reach their trading decisions tend to prefer margined FX.

The downside is that margined FX tends to be slightly more expensive than CFD trading. In addition, some brokerages will limit the lifespan of their contracts, which means your trade could be in danger of expiring before you're ready. CFDs and spread bets, meanwhile, are more likely to be rolled over (with a small cost attached).

Spot foreign exchange

As with margined FX trading (above), spot FX involves trading in the *real* market. You are buying and selling *real* currency. Spot FX does not necessarily involve trading on margin, however. This is more a game for traders with very large quantities of cash to invest, who don't want the additional headache of financing charges or margin calls.

There is more emphasis here on your base currency. While with a CFD or spread bet account you can have your trading capital in GBP and still trade USD/CHF, if you're trading spot FX your base currency is important. It is probably less of an issue if your capital is denominated in US dollars and you are speculating against the other currency majors, but in the event you want to trade GBP/EUR you have a problem.

One way of getting round this is via an FX swap arrangement, whereby your broker lends you another currency for the trade.

Effectively, you lend some money to your broker in one currency and he lends you the currency you need for the trade. The swap – for that is what it is, a swapping of one currency for another – is at a fixed rate and brings with it the obligation to swap back again at a certain date in the future.

Thus, if you were a USD investor and needed EUR to trade some third currency pairs, like EUR/JPY or GBP/EUR, you could swap USD for EUR to give you a EUR war chest. You would just need to make sure your euro positions were closed out before the swap expired.

Futures contracts

If you have a futures trading account, you can also trade FX futures. The futures markets grew originally out of the agriculture and shipping markets, and were based on the need of some consumers of commodities to take delivery of a certain product at a specific time in the future, hence the name. The commodities futures market is very large and very liquid; the currencies futures market, by contrast, is tiny compared with the vast size of spot FX.

Currency futures are exchange-traded contracts that allow you to speculate on where you think a currency pair might stand at some point in the future. All futures contracts have an expiry date, usually at the end of a given month. As the contract approaches its expiry date, it will tend to converge on the underlying spot price.

Futures contracts will tend to be quoted with tighter spreads than other types of currency trading account. In addition, you will tend to see lower transaction costs and higher levels of available leverage. However, the futures markets usually require much larger minimum trade sizes (USD25,000+ for a single lot is typical, although this can be bought on margin). In addition, they can be traded only when the futures exchange is open, so you lose the benefit of the 24-hour interbank currency market.

Because the futures market is not as 'deep' as the interbank market, the price of contracts can also be moved substantially by aggressive buying or selling. Futures markets, while they are traded by speculators, also serve the needs of institutions seeking to hedge their currency risk, often to the tune of millions of dollars.

Options

Trading currency options is slightly different to futures. An option contract lets you buy or sell at a specific price either at or before a pre-set date. You pay a small premium for the option contract that you will lose regardless of whether you exercise the option.

A **put** option lets you sell something at a given price, while a **call** lets you buy it. So, if you think the market is going to go up, and you want to be able to buy it at a cheaper level, a call option is what you want. If, however, you think the market will fall, then a put option lets you lock in a higher price than the one you expect will prevail in the future.

If EUR/USD, for example, was trading at $1.410 and you expected it to go to $1.600, you could buy a call option on EUR/USD at $1.460, for example. This would let you buy the euro at $1.460 and sell it at $1.600 (if you were right, of course, and the EUR did climb).

If EUR/USD was at $1.410 and you expected it to fall, you'd go shopping for a put option that would let you sell euro at $1.450 (or higher). That way you could buy the euro at a cheaper price in the market and then sell it for a higher one.

An option, like a future, has a specific lifetime. At some point, if it is not exercised, the option will expire. In the options market, your counterparty is providing you with the right to buy (or sell) something up until or at a specific date. Once that date is reached, it is worthless and expires. It is not like a future, especially a commodity future, where you might be expected to actually take delivery of an asset. An option just disappears like morning dew.

Options come in two different types: American-style, which can be exercised whenever you want, and European-style, which can be exercised only on the expiry date. Most FX options are European style.

Also bear in mind that, as with other types of currency trades, there are two sides to a currency options contract. If I am buying a call option on EUR/USD, by definition I'm also buying a put on the USD.

The options described above are the simple vanilla option. There are also more complex varieties on offer to the FX trader.

If you are reading this in the UK or Ireland, it is also possible to spread bet tax free on options prices. You will need to shop around for the right broker for this.

Forwards

A currency forward is a little more predictable than a future. You agree to buy or sell a currency at a specific rate at a date in the future. Traditional FX forwards are available to buy or sell with maturities from two days up to about two years into the future.

A forward contract is usually based off the spot value of the currency pair, which in turn is established a couple of business days *after* the actual trade date. The attraction of the forward is that you are guaranteeing a trade at a specific date at a specific rate. It is a type of trade favoured by risk-averse market participants who like to hedge their currency risk, protecting themselves against price fluctuations in the interim.

If you want to be able to buy or sell $10,000 at a rate near its current rate but in a month from now, the forward could be the contract for you. The forward is less attractive for currency traders who are just in the market to exploit price differences. If you take a view on a currency, and want to be able to buy or sell it more expensively or more cheaply at a specific time in the future, it may be cheaper to go with an option. Forwards are more suited to investors who want to strip out the volatility of currency markets from their activity.

Forwards are OTC derivatives: like a CFD you are trading with a counterparty, not with an exchange or in the interbank market. You are exposing yourself to a degree of credit risk, because there is the obligation on both sides to execute the second part of the deal at the agreed date: if one of them goes bankrupt, the other can be left out of pocket.

Currency forwards are less popular with retail traders. While activity in spot FX, CFDs, margined FX and futures is growing, forwards seem to have less appeal to the private investors unless they are involved in big transactions in other assets and need to hedge their currency risk.

Currency ETFs

Currency exchange-traded funds (ETFs) are funds that are listed on a stock exchange and trade like a share. They can usually be bought and sold through a stock broker like other shares. They are based on independently published indexes which track the performance of a single currency against either the USD or the EUR. These can include emerging markets currencies as well.

ETFs allow you to buy into the performance of a currency using a share-trading account, but you won't be benefiting from the same levels of leverage as you might with a margined FX account.

The main attraction of currency ETFs is that they are segregated: if the issuing firm fails, investor assets are still protected. Because these are funds, holders of ETFs are charged an annual management fee as they would be with a unit trust or mutual fund, although such fees tend to be lower than those charged for actively managed funds.

Finally, you can now buy leveraged currency ETFs which give you enhanced performance, akin to CFDs or margined FX but not quite as devastating. The investor will usually be offered ×2 or ×3 the price movement.

Different types of trades

There are a number of different types of online FX contract now available, particularly being offered by companies that have spread bets or CFDs as part of their product range. Which you use will depend partly on what your chosen provider is offering but also on what suits you best as a trader.

As the retail FX industry has matured and evolved, so enterprising firms have sought new ways to accommodate their customers and win new business from their competitors. This has led to increasing product innovation in this space, which at times may be confusing for the beginner. Don't be daunted, however: once you have found the type of trade that suits you, you will probably find yourself sticking to it.

Daily trades

These are short-term FX trades which expire at the end of the day. You can buy them at any point during the trading day, and they will tend to reflect the underlying cash market or spot price. They are easier to get to grips with than futures-based trades, but they do expire at the day-end. They obviously suit the more short-term trader who is looking at intra-day movements in the market.

Rolling trades

More recently, brokerages have been offering their clients rolling trades, effectively a daily trade which you are able to 'roll over' every night, usually for a small charge. Rolling trades let you keep your position open indefinitely. They can become quite expensive over time, as the ongoing daily financing charges build up, but for the trader that is comfortable with a very short-term time horizon, they are quite useful.

There are other types of bets now being made available, some of which are exclusive to certain firms or are less widely available than those mentioned above.

Binary bets/trades

Binary bets are 'all or nothing bets' based like spread bets on movements in financial markets. A binary bet asks you to decide whether a currency will close above or below a specific level. It may even be quoted with a certain time of day.

The price of a binary bet will not resemble the price of the currency pair itself. Remember, you are betting only on whether it closes up or down, so the actual price has less relevance. The number quoted should be subtracted from 100 and the total multiplied by your stake.

Example

A binary bet on the EUR/USD might be quoted at 19/24 for 1.21042. If you staked $10 that the pair would be up at the bet's expiry (i.e. above 1.21042), you would be using the offer price of 24. If the market is over 1.21042 as the bet expires, you would win $100 − 24 = 76$ ($×$10$) = $760.

If, however, the market was down, your loss would be calculated as $24 × 10 = 240.

As you can see, you lose much more than your original stake if you are wrong. However, your potential losses are more limited in a way because you define your maximum loss at the outset when you determine your stake.

Binaries are available over differing time frames: you can bet on where the currency will be in five minutes or in a week, for example. The range of currencies is more limited for the more short-term bets, but the popularity of binary betting has meant that many companies have been adding to the available markets over the last couple of years. In addition, you can bet on key economic indicators, such as interest rates or US Non-Farm Payrolls, which is impractical for a standard exchange-cleared or spot FX contract.

Binary spreads will tend to be less than eight points, another factor that makes them attractive to traders.

Apart from the conventional win/lose binary bet, brokerages now offer some new takes on the binary format, including:

- *Target bets:* the bet pays out if the currency closes up or down within a certain range. You might be betting on whether the bet will expire when the market is up 50–70 points, for example. If it expires north of the range, of course, the bet won't pay out.

- *Tunnel bets:* here you are betting the market will remain within a specific range during the life of the bet. If the market trades outside this band at any time during the lifetime of the bet, you lose. If the bet expires without the market having traded outside the range, you win. This is a good way to make money if a market is range-bound, but do look out for the break.

- *One-touch bets:* the bet pays out if the market ever goes through a nominated target level during the lifetime of the bet. It does not need to expire above the given level, just breach it.

- *High/Low (or 'Hi Lo') bets:* these are bets usually based on what the market does today. You are betting on whether the high point or the low point is a given distance (or more) from the previous day's closing point. For instance, you might bet that the high point today will be 50 pips higher by the time the bet expires. You are less worried about what the closing price is, so long as at some point the high is beyond 50 points.

All the above are OTC trades: they are really bets, with the broker acting as your counterparty or bookie. Some traders like them because of their structured nature, and especially because it lets them take a view on economic reports without risking larger sums of capital via a CFD for example. The fact that you can define your acceptable loss and keep it to that is another selling point.

DIY bets

Also called custom bets, these are a potentially fast-growing and exciting development in the world of FX and the wider world of trading as well. It is more suited to the short-term market strategy, but it gives the trader more control over what the parameters are for the bet itself, particularly in the all-important risk quotient.

Custom betting seems to be geared more towards the short-term trader who is looking to make money off small, possibly intra-day movements in the market. It might be worth looking at if you are thinking more about multiple trades in and out of the market during a single day. Like binary bets, it is easier to nominate how much money you want to risk, and you are less likely to lose unforeseen quantities as the consequence of sudden market movements. It is a bit like binary betting, but here you have a bit more control over what you'd like to bet on (and the broker will then quote you the price).

With the increased popularity of betting exchanges, which have expanded the scope of how and on what traders can now bet, it seems that this area of the market is destined to grow as well.

Are custom betting and binary betting real trading? In some respects, it feels more like a trip to the bookie – you are simply betting on financial markets rather than on horses or football. But at the same time, financial markets can be slightly more predictable. There is an argument that a skilled trader could still make money using binary bets if he was used to intra-day trading and had a good feel for the market he was betting on. He might see a trend emerging but still with a degree of uncertainty about it. He might therefore feel it was worth opening a binary trade which limited his risk, rather than a conventional trade.

Finding the right company to trade with

Many experienced traders have more than one trading account. There are a number of good reasons for doing this, and if you can afford it, it can be worth doing. FX companies come in all shapes and sizes. Most will offer the same core range of currency markets, but beyond that there are many ways to differentiate them. Before opening an account, it is worth shopping around using the criteria that are important for you.

More forex brokerages are springing up all the time, and the competition for new accounts is becoming fiercer. In addition, some of the major companies allow their trading platforms to be white-labelled by partners, including banks, stock brokers and independent financial advisers. This means more and more people around the world are being offered the chance to trade FX. Most of the time, all these trades are being channelled through the same handful of brokerage firms.

The failure in 2011 of MF Global, one of the biggest brokerages on the street, following what seems to have been a bad trade on the European sovereign debt market, has illustrated some of the hidden risks in FX trading. It demonstrates that even the largest brokerages can be prone to sudden and catastrophic failure. Under these circumstances, it is better to spread your risk across multiple brokers than to have all your trading capital frozen when a brokerage gets into trouble.

The increasing number of firms offering FX trading at the retail level is still good news for you, the private trader, because it means you are able to shop around for the best account for your purposes. It is worth doing some background research on companies on the internet, or checking out independent websites like The Armchair Trader (www. thearmchairtrader.com), which have plenty of information on what exactly the various companies are offering, allowing you to weigh them against each other.

What's in a price?

Although you may see a price quoted for currencies online from a variety of sources, this will not necessarily be the price you see on your trading screen, or the price you will be able to execute at. Why?

Trading companies are like market makers in the real stock market. They 'make' a price on a financial market for you to trade. They are starting to provide some traders with what is called Direct Market Access (DMA), but in reality there are two entities which sit between you, the trader, and the global foreign exchange markets. There is no real 'official' price for a currency pair that is internationally recognised: banks and other major market participants will work with each other to try to arrive at what the consensus bid/offer price for a particular pair is at any moment in time. Technology is helping with this process, so pricing is becoming more efficient, but it can be difficult at times for a trader to properly evaluate what the right price should be for a currency pair at any given moment in time.

If you are trading futures or margined FX with DMA to the interbank market, then the prices you are using should be more accurate and stick with the tick-by-tick reality of that currency pair. This is because your broker is quoting you actual interbank prices, albeit with his spread built in (if he has one). The alternative is he quotes you the interbank spread and then charges you a commission. With futures, of course, you are trading an exchange-cleared derivative. However, with CFDs and spread bets you are trading on the price quoted to you by the broker.

Between the interbank FX market and the spread betting or CFD company you deal with sits another beast, usually an investment bank acting as a prime broker. An FX brokerage may use several prime brokers to give it access to currency markets in order to find the best price in the market. With spread betting or CFD trading specifically, while you may feel as though you are trading the market, and the price may be very similar to the one you are seeing quoted elsewhere, the price is ultimately the one your broker chooses to quote you. *The broker is under no obligation to quote you the same price you are seeing in the market*; they will quote you the price of their product which tracks the market, but this will not be a product that matches the market pip for pip. Indeed, it is hard even for professionals to find a 'true' market price from their brokers.

Prime brokers will quote prices on markets to retail brokers, but the price quoted by Deutsche Bank will not necessarily be the same price quoted by Goldman Sachs or Credit Suisse. They will be close, but not the same. The broker then needs to come up with their own price, based on what it would theoretically get in the market. A good policy would be to aim for a price somewhere in the middle of those quoted by the prime brokers, but your broker is under no obligation to do so, and depending on the level of automation involved in its pricing processes, you may see some substantial deviation from the spot price quoted in the market.

On top of this, you have to factor in the spread. As your broker is quoting two prices, a bid and an offer, and each company has its own set of spreads, you can end up seeing some wide variations in prices, particularly during periods of high market volatility.

Finally, it is also worth remembering that the price quoted is not necessarily the price at which your order will be executed. Again, it ought to be, and with very small trades it usually is. Suffice it to say that if you find most of your trades are being filled at a different price from what you were quoted, it may be time to start looking for another broker.

Demo accounts

Many companies will offer you the capability to do some trading with no money at all using a demonstration or 'demo' account, and I would encourage you to do this for a while, in order to get comfortable not only with the processes involved but also with the platform you are using to trade on. You can do this before opening a live account. Some companies will offer you only a limited number of markets to trade on, or will let you have access for a limited period of time – two weeks, for example.

There is one big difference with demo accounts, however: you will never have any problems with liquidity. Your buy and sell trades will always be met because, at the end of the day, this is just a sophisticated computer game until you put some real money in. Nobody at the other end is having to hedge any market exposure. This can create the illusion that you will always be able to buy and sell at the price you want, but in live trading conditions this will not always be possible.

3

Risk management for the forex trader

Risk should always be foremost in the mind of anybody trading currencies. When traders get a position wrong, be they private traders or the professionals, more often than not it is because they get their risk management wrong. Many, many investors who plunge into FX trading pay little attention to risk, or simply do not understand the sorts of risks they are taking on. They end up losing money, become downhearted, close their accounts, and go on to do something else.

Trading foreign exchange markets is not like investing in a mutual fund. Opening a trade and letting it run without having adequate built-in protection can cost you a lot of money. Nobody else is going to pay attention to your active positions. It is up to you to come up with an adequate risk framework, and to go from there.

Professional money managers spend a lot of time talking about risk, seeking to quantify it, and using phrases like 'dial up on the risk' or 'taking risk off the table'. You may also read in the financial press about the market becoming more 'risk averse'. Trading currency markets is all about confidence and awareness of risk. The last thing you want, as a trader, is to be ambushed by an unforeseen risk.

Margin trading

Forex trading frequently involves trading on margin – many investors see margin facilities as the easiest way to make a considerable profit from changes in currency markets, but these markets can be a two-edged sword. We discussed the basics of margin trading earlier in this book, but it pays to revisit the inherent risks involved in trading on margin, as this sets online currency trading apart from investing in shares or investment trusts.

Margin trading in effect means borrowing money to trade. Imagine if a bank lent you money to trade rather than buy a new car. The bank says it will let you pocket any profits or losses. By lending you $50,000, it allows you to make bigger profits – or losses – than you would be able to do with $5,000.

Margin trading works very like this. The bank here is the FX bro-kerage. It asks you to provide a portion of the trade – say 10 per cent – and it effectively 'lends' you the rest. Trading companies pay a lot of attention to the creditworthiness of their clientele and for obvious reasons: if someone loses more money than they have on deposit with the firm, they want to be sure that the trader can still cover his losses.

Forex brokerages like CFD companies and spread betting firms set margin rates that will differ depending upon the market. The rate reflects to a large extent the cost to the brokerage of hedging its underlying risk in the market. The more liquid the market, the lower the margin is likely to be. Liquidity is a very important consideration for the online trader: it represents how easy it is to buy and sell some-thing in the market. Luckily, FX markets are among the most liquid markets there are, so you are likely to see tiny margins required for most currency markets.

You will tend to see the same low margins quoted across most of the big FX pairs, but if something affects the liquidity of the financial system, as occurred in 2008, you could see margins rocket upwards very quickly indeed. Brokerages are under no obligation to continue to quote you a 1 per cent margin on GBP/USD indefinitely. The same goes for spreads on currency pairs – usually these will remain static, but in some cases they can widen suddenly, particularly with the smaller, less liquid currencies. Be alive to the fact that a currency broker can broaden a spread any time it likes.

The lower-margin markets will tend to be the most liquid. Thus, you should see 1–5 per cent margin asked for forex markets. These markets are very liquid, as they are based on the huge volumes traded in the interbank market every day.

On the face of it, margin trading sounds like a great idea. After all, your bank is unlikely to lend you money to gamble with. And you are risking only a small fraction of the total trade, yet you get to keep all the profits.

The problem here is that you also carry the losses. Think of a margin trade like a high-performance sports car – you can drive a lot faster, but when you crash, you are risking life and limb. That is why most FX brokerages are obliged by their regulator to publish risk warnings on their marketing literature and their websites. It is therefore essential to keep a close eye on how trading on margin can affect your profits and losses.

In Figure 3.1 you can see how margin can turbo-charge the potential profits you can make from a trade, in this case using just 1 per cent margin to trade EUR/USD. The column on the left is the trade using physical currency, with no margin involved. The column on the right is the trade with the margin factored in – i.e. a typical margined FX trade. Here we are assuming a small gain in the currency of 1.5 per cent – you can see how, with margin trading, your profit potential is magnified.

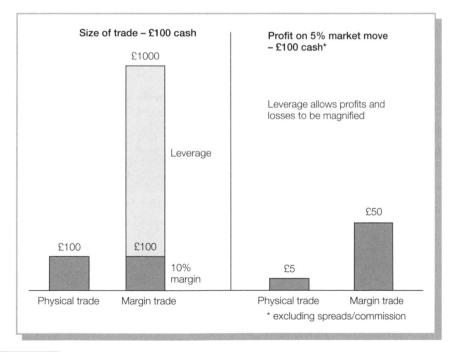

Figure 3.1   Profit potential of margin trading

Now imagine that same trade in reverse. Figure 3.2 gives you some idea of what a 1.5 per cent loss would look like. The third column illustrates the total 'weight' or risk you are wearing. You can see that by margin trading you are effectively 'owning' a much bigger amount of risk. The brokerage may be lending you the money to trade with, but the profit or loss is all yours, come what may.

Consequently, FX trading requires much closer day-to-day monitoring of your positions, and this is why many traders prefer to close out all their positions when they go away on holiday, or even when they go to sleep, despite the 24-hour nature of global currency markets – they don't like to have the additional psychological pressure of open trades to keep them awake.

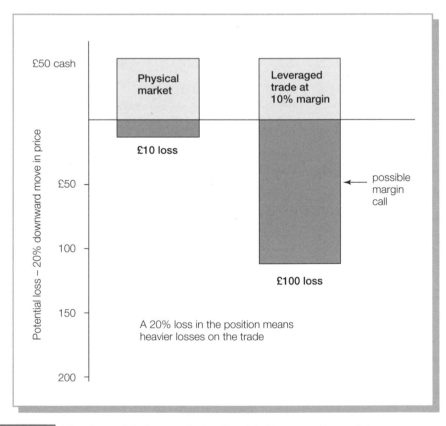

Figure 3.2   The downside to margin trading (at 10 per cent margin)

Stop losses

Most online FX brokerages should now provide you with the ability to place 'stop losses'. They will let you insert an automatic sell order when you open the bet, or indeed later on (some are now insisting that traders automatically have a stop loss in place when they open a trade). The stop loss sets the price at which the company will close the position, and is often used as a key tool in risk management. It means you have a degree of peace of mind: your trade will not keep losing you money; at some point it will be closed. It lets you define how much money you are prepared to lose on a given trade.

It is important, when putting a stop in place, that you do not place it too close to where you opened the trade. Otherwise you can quickly be 'stopped out' of that trade when you don't really need to be.

In Figure 3.3 you can see an hourly chart of the USD/JPY, with the yen weakening against the dollar. You can see how a trade has been opened and two hypothetical stops have been put in place. Stop A was too close to the market, and in this case the trader loses some of the potential profits he could have pocketed later on. Stop B is set further off the market – the trader is taking on more risk and the potential for a bigger loss if the stop is hit, but he also makes more profit under this scenario as his trade stays live, and he profits from more of the upside in the market.

Assessing where to place stops really depends on the volatility of the currency market you are betting on and the timescale you are using. Not only does the volatility of markets change constantly, but some markets are inherently more volatile than others. Some traders love volatile currency markets because they feel they can make more money when the price is moving in big jumps, while others seek out steady, consistent trends over a period of days or weeks.

It is important that you have a good feel for the potential price jumps of a currency pair you are trading. Think about your timescale first. Are you a short-term trader or a longer-term trader? How long do you

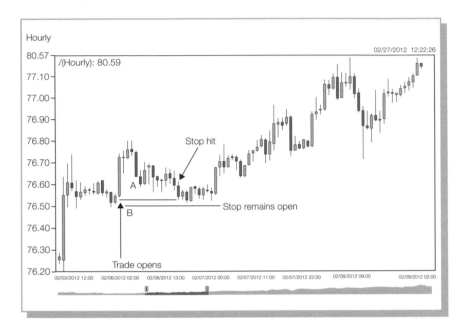

Source: Adapted from www.forexpros.com

Figure 3.3   **Placing stop losses**

expect the bet to be open, and do you have any particular target price you would like to reach?

Then look at what the price of that pair has done over the time period under review, but go back further, too. How has it behaved? Think of it like a person: what does its temperament look like? Is it subject to sudden and unpredictable jumps? Even if you expect to be in the market for no more than a week, it is worth tracking back several weeks to see where the price has gone in the past. You don't want to be surprised by a sudden change of mood, even if the last temper tantrum was a few weeks or even months ago (see Figures 3.4 and 3.5).

This is no guarantee of future market behaviour, of course, but it can provide useful information about where to place your stops without them being hit immediately.

Source: www.forexpros.com

Figure 3.4   Example of a quiet market

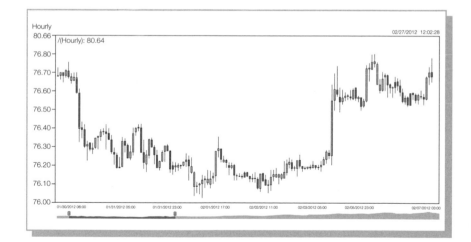

Source: www.forexpros.com

Figure 3.5   Example of a temperamental market

Source: www.forexpros.com

Figure 3.6   Informed stop losses

Figure 3.6 gives another example, this time of the USD/JPY currency pair. You can see how, by looking back over a period of a couple of months, the trader can assess whether the price is likely to move suddenly, and places his stops accordingly.

Placing stop losses can also be informed by technical analysis. We will look at this in more detail in Chapter 8, but technical analysis can certainly help to keep you abreast of where to put your stops. You can see from looking at Figure 3.7, that the currency pair hits a number of resistance levels, both on the way up and on the way down. We will discuss resistance levels in more detail in Chapter 8, but suffice to say resistance levels are predictable turning points in a given price. They can also help you when deciding where to put your stop losses.

When is a stop loss *really* a stop loss?

Bear in mind that a stop loss does not necessarily guarantee that your trade will be closed at that price. Your brokerage will use that stop loss as an indicator and will try to close the trade as soon as it can once that price point is reached. Only if the company offers its clients *guaranteed* stop losses can you expect to see trades closed at the price you want.

Some traders complain vociferously about trades not being closed efficiently. This really boils down to a question of quality of service more than anything else. As the technological infrastructure underpinning the way forex brokerages manage their client accounts becomes more efficient, I expect to see more firms offering guaranteed stop losses as a standard part of their service package.

The other big complaint is that companies deliberately stop their clients out. The argument here is that currency brokerages might know that a large number of clients have stops in place at a certain level and can 'twitch' the price down far enough to trigger all the stops. This does happen in the real market from time to time as well. If you are trading using a spread betting or CFD account, the prices you trade on are the prices quoted by the company itself, *not* the real market (although an effort is made to keep them as close together as possible), and consequently there is always a suspicion in the minds of some traders that they are being deliberately stopped out.

I cannot say for certain that this is regular practice in currency trading; I've certainly not seen it happen myself. Ultimately, forex brokerages will make money if they see more volume, not if they punish their customers' risk management strategies. They are waking up to the fact that an unhappy customer is a customer who won't trade with them any longer. The days of 'churn and burn' in retail trading are fast disappearing. Still, if you feel unhappy with the service you are getting on your stop losses, take it up with the firm or close your account and trade with someone else.

Trailing stop losses

Trailing stop losses are coming into increasing use in retail FX trading and represent a potentially profitable innovation for traders. With a trailing stop the stop loss moves behind the price. You simply decide how far behind. This way you can potentially lock in profits once the trailing stop has passed the point where you entered the market. If the price falls back, it will hit the stop at a much higher level than if it was merely static. The stop itself will not move if the price goes into reverse – it moves only when the price goes in your favour. It is there to protect you against any downside.

Figure 3.7 illustrates the difference between a trailing stop and a static stop, using the EUR/USD. As you can see, while the static stop protects our trader against some of the falls in the market, he is also losing out on some potential upside profits in the process.

Don't forget that the spreads on some currency trades can widen suddenly, for example on the back of an unexpected currency intervention by a central bank. Not all spreads will remain the same all the time, particularly if you are trading emerging markets currencies as opposed to the major currency pairs like EUR/USD or USD/JPY. If your stop loss is too close to the price, a sudden widening of the spread can trigger your stop.

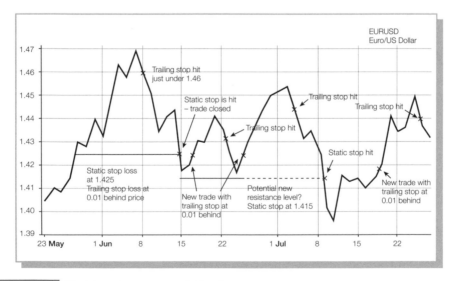

Figure 3.7   Trailing stop versus static stop

One other important point to bear in mind when using stop losses: some firms' trading platforms can also treat the stop as an order to open a new trade, so be sure that, once you close a trade manually, the stop is also closed. Otherwise, if your live trade is gone and the stop is still there, and the price moves through it later on, a new trade can be opened automatically. It sounds silly, but it pays to be sure.

Let's say you were long the US dollar against the yen and had a stop loss in place, but then saw the market coming off yourself and decided to close the trade. With some companies, if the USD/JPY then fell through your still-existing stop, a short trade would open and you would be live in the market with a short position. This happens far too often and is the cause of many complaints to brokerages: the trading platform is automated and will simply take your instruction as a signal to open a new trade. Make sure you remove any unused stops as they can cost you a lot of money.

Under these circumstances, you would be notified as per usual that a new trade was live, but it is very important that you are familiar with the way stop losses are treated by the firm you are trading with in order to avoid this. Some firms cancel stops when you close the bet, others don't.

Managing your exposure

It is critical, when trading on margin, that you have sufficient cash to cover any losses you take. This means not just the deposit but any other losses that might occur. After all, one of the big differences between trading on margin and trading assets in the physical market – such as listed shares or investment trusts – is that you really can lose more money than you put up. If things go badly, £100 of initial risk can quickly turn into a much larger loss, particularly if there are no stops in place and the market turns suddenly and unexpectedly against you.

Each firm will also calculate its margin requirement differently. Increasingly, some FX trading firms are keeping their customers abreast of what their total margin requirement is. This will be the amount of money you will need to have on deposit to meet your share of an open trade.

Some brokerages will use winning trades or other positions as positive factors in calculating your total margin requirement, while others will factor in any stops you have in place, but it is best to ask what the margin policy is before diving in, particularly if your total margin requirement is not immediately apparent on your trading screen. Increasingly, more trading firms are reporting total margin required on a real-time basis, which is a big help for traders who can't take the time out to calculate their margin every couple of hours. It can become increasingly complicated if several positions are open at the same time.

Your margin will change as the value of open positions changes. If you start losing money, your brokerage is entitled to ask you to deposit more cash in your account ('a margin call'). If you don't, or are unable to, then they are within their rights to start closing your positions themselves and saddling you with a loss.

Most experienced traders will keep a substantial amount of cash in their account ready to meet the margin requirements of any trades which might start losing ground. What they don't do is risk 80 per cent of their trading capital as margin on open trades and hope for the best. This still happens to a surprisingly large degree, even among those who depend on trading for their living. They still consistently commit too much money to the market, and this inevitably leads to their downfall when unexpected circumstances occur. Trading requires discipline, and it also requires trading capital for this very reason.

FX brokerages always advise clients not to risk money that they cannot afford to lose. It helps a trader's peace of mind if he knows he can get wiped out and it won't have a knock-on effect on his life-style! Ploughing your life savings or university money into a trading account in the hopes of growing it quickly almost always ends in tears.

It is also worth getting out of the market from time to time, partly from a psychological perspective, but also if you are going to be out of touch with your computer for an extended period of time. I know of one Swiss-based trader who every year closes out all her positions at the end of June and then goes travelling around Asia for a couple of months. This lets her get away from the markets at a time when they're relatively quiet, but at the same time she can do some important thinking about the strategies she employs, and she always finds she can bring something new to her approach when she returns to Switzerland in the autumn.

Mobile trading applications are making it easier for traders to keep tabs on their positions on the move, but these are no excuse for poor risk management. Any serious break from the currency markets should include 'going to cash' and exiting all positions. It means you don't have to worry about bad things happening to your account while you are away, and you can relax on the beach without having to steal a glance at the markets every day (unless you want to, of course).

When starting out, then, it is worth only ever having one or two positions open at the same time and making sure you keep abreast of your margin exposure on a day-by-day basis.

Position sizing

Seasoned currency traders will not risk all their money in active trades. Indeed, they will tend to commit only a tiny proportion of the money they have on deposit with the broker – as little as 1–3 per cent. This means an account with £5,000 might be using only £150 on a single live trade. This is sometimes referred to as the Pot Risk Rule. It is designed to protect you against a string of bad losses.

It seems very conservative to be risking only £150 at a time when have you £5,000 sitting in your account, but this is the reality of good risk management in today's trading world. Under this rule, if you lost that £150, you would then have only £4,850 to bet with. Your next maximum trade would be around £145. As you can see, if you were particularly unlucky and took a string of hits to your trading capital, you would be risking progressively less on each trade. What you would *not* be doing is putting more risk on the table in order to make up for previous losses – this is the road to eventual trading disaster.

Under this conservative scenario, it may seem like it will take you for ever to make any money trading currency markets, and certainly that dream of perhaps one day trading by the pool of your villa in Spain may seem even further out of reach, but bear in mind you are also using leverage here. Even with £150, at 1 per cent margin your total market position would be £15,000.

Position sizing also helps you to evaluate your stop losses. If you are betting with a maximum loss per trade of £150, you will be able to see which markets are too volatile for your current risk tolerance. You don't want to be spread betting in a market which regularly sweeps through 100 points if you are betting £2 per point.

Not all currency trades are created equal

When trading forex, you are allocating risk against a currency pair and will make or lose money according to how many pips that currency moves through. Some currencies move around more than others and can go through periods of volatility, basically the degree to which the price of that currency fluctuates against another. Traders often like volatility because it means there is the potential to make a lot of money in a short period of time – so long as they get it right, of course.

The volatility of different currencies will tend to change over time. There are periods when the currency markets will seem quite quiet, for instance when traders are away from their desks over Christmas; at other times they can be particularly busy. Recent EU summits to discuss the future of the euro have provoked plenty of speculative activity in EUR currency pairs.

Source: www.forexpros.com

Figure 3.8   USD/PLN Oct/Nov 2011

Because some currencies move through such wide swings, it is important that you take this into consideration when you are setting your stops.

Not all pips are created equally, either. Most currencies are quoted to four or five decimal points. Any currency quoted in terms of USD – the right-hand currency is USD – will usually be to five decimal points, with a pip value of $10. This makes it easy to work out how much a position is changing in value.

In Figure 3.8 we have an emerging markets currency pair experiencing high volatility. Take into consideration the number of pips this market moves by. The Polish zloty gained by 3,500 pips against the US dollar between the end of September 2011 and the last week of October.

Consider this example, using a simple spot trade in the market – no margin involved:

£10,000 of USD/PLN sold (offer) at 3.55000 (short trade on the USD/PLN pair).

Because we have five figures quoted to the right of the decimal place, we're effectively risking a pound for each pip the price moves.

USD/PLN bought (bid) at 3.47500

Profit = 0.07500 x £10,000 = £750

Remember, if you had been trading on margin, you would have been using far less of your own money, maybe only £100 at 1 per cent margin, but you would still have been looking at a big loss if you got it wrong. Your stops would have had to have been set much wider.

In Figure 3.9 we have a less volatile pair, namely the GBP/EUR rate. Here we can see a strong move by sterling from the beginning of December, when it is just above 1.60000, to over 1.21000 at the beginning of January 2012. It is a move of just over 39,000 pips.

Again:

£10,000 of GBP/EUR bought (bid) at 1.60020

GBP/EUR sold (offer) at 1.21020

Profit = 0.39000 x 10,000 = £3,900.

Here we see less volatility – the pair fell into a bit of a tight trading range from about the 14th of December, but this was predictable as traders and central bankers were all away on their Christmas holidays. As you can see, it picks up again after New Year.

However, it is important to note that the profit potential, and the risk, is much reduced in the GBP/EUR market. For starters, it is not an emerging markets currency, and much more heavily traded than, say, the PLN. Second, a more conservative stop loss of, say, 120 pips would not have been hit. Stops can thus be a lot closer to the price in this market.

Make sure you have a back-up plan

Beyond the risks you take on with margin trading in the market, there are unforeseen risks that might impact your trading strategy and for which it can be useful to have a plan. What happens, for example, if you lose your internet connection, or you spill your coffee on your computer and it shorts out? What is your back-up plan?

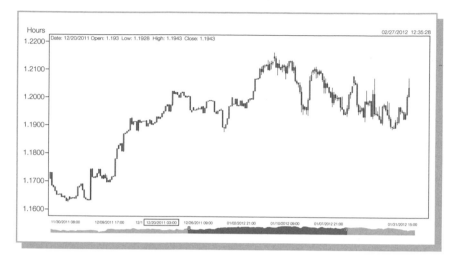

Date: 12/20/2011 Open: 1.193 Low: 1.1928 High: 1.1943 Close: 1.1943   02/27/2012 12:35:28

Source: www.forexpros.com

Figure 3.9 **GBP/EUR Nov 2011/Jan 2012**

It is worth thinking about these key risks early on so that you have a plan in place should something like this happen. Problems with technology are often cited, but there are other questions, such as your ability to trade. What happens if you are taken ill suddenly, with live positions in the market? Is anyone authorised to close your trades for you if this happens?

If your brokerage – your counterparty in industry parlance – should fail, it is worth knowing what your recourse is. After the events of 2008, when queues formed outside branches of the Northern Rock building society, many traders and investors became much more cautious about who their counterparties were. In the wake of the collapse of Lehman Brothers the same year, it seems as if no financial institution is theoretically too big to fail, and as a trader you won't know which banks your trading company is exposed to.

The failure with the most direct impact on traders in recent history has been MF Global, the spin-out from Man Group, which collapsed in 2011. While it was strongly positioned in commodities markets, MF Global also had spread betting and CFD trading arms in several countries. Its unexpected demise left many traders with their capital locked up in the company, often with trades still live in the market, at the mercy of the administrators. At the time of writing, many traders were still waiting to see funds released, and while some accounts had been transferred to other brokerages, margin deposits had not.

The best protection under these circumstances is to use more than one counterparty, and if you can afford it, split your trading cash between them. It will mean you can't trade some markets, which have to be a bit tighter in terms of your overall margin, but this is no bad thing, particularly for the beginner.

When trading companies fail

Under normal market conditions, it is unlikely that FX brokerages will fail, but under extreme circumstances, as we saw in 2008 and more recently with the collapse of MF Global, trading firms can get into difficulties with their own creditors, and can collapse.

Echelon Fund Management was a Scotland-based spread betting firm which collapsed in 2008 with debts of more than £30 million as its credit lines were severed. This was happening to a lot of companies in 2008, not just spread betting firms, but Echelon was forced to close its doors when a major creditor in Switzerland turned off the taps. Approximately 900 Echelon clients ended up as creditors of the now-insolvent spread betting firm. Under these circumstances, because Echelon was regulated by the UK regulator, the Financial Services Authority (FSA), its spread betting clients were entitled to recompense to the tune of up to £48,000 each. This was because spread betting companies in the UK are covered by the Investors Compensation Scheme.

Smaller trading concerns are also more vulnerable to big losses being run up by their own clients. Companies will sometimes have blue-chip clients who trade large sums of money. They need to keep a close eye on them because it is possible for large losses sustained by a single customer to bring down the whole firm, as happened to Global Trader Europe (GTE) in 2008. In the case of GTE, the losses caused a shortfall in the minimum amount of regulatory capital, which the firm is obliged to keep on deposit to meet FSA requirements. Its South African parent company took the decision not to continue to support it, forcing it out of business.

Smaller firms are much more prone to collapse than their bigger cousins, and it seems that periods of market volatility and uncertainty can increase this risk. The fall of MF Global in 2011 is arguably the largest single instance of a major brokerage with retail clients going to the wall. Retail traders have ended up in exactly the same position as many institutional clients of MF Global. Because it was an international operation, with offices as far afield as Chicago and Sydney, MF Global's subsequent break-up is being handled according to the prevailing law and regulatory environment in each country. Hence, traders in Singapore seem to be getting their money back faster than traders in the US.

One of the controversies that arose from the case of MF Global has been the way client funds are managed. Some regulators, like those in the UK and the US, insist that client money is segregated, making it easy to calculate who is owed what in the case of the collapse of a big brokerage. However, this seems not to have been the case in Australia. At the time of writing details were still being established, but it seemed that MF Global had been pooling client funds in Australia for the purposes of hedging, using a regulatory loophole in that country.

When the dust settles from MF Global, there will undoubtedly be more scrutiny on the way brokerages around the world manage client accounts. It always, always pays, however, to make sure you have more than one trading account. Don't put all your eggs in one basket. Shop around and use two or more brokers, even if this means you don't have as much capital on tap and might find some markets are beyond the reach of your trading resources as a consequence. This also lets you compare the prices and speed of execution of each firm. If a brokerage is not coming up to scratch, close your account and go somewhere else.

When opening an FX trading account, always check to see who regulates your counterparty. In the age of online trading, it is becoming increasingly easy to open an account with companies in different countries, particularly if you live somewhere where the domestic financial services industry is underdeveloped. An internet connection can quickly put you in touch with brokerages across the planet, and the 24-hour nature of FX trading in particular means that many of these firms never stand still. But make sure you check who regulates them, as this will give you some idea of what your recourse will be should a brokerage fail.

If a brokerage is based – and regulated – in a country where you suspect the local financial authorities may not be up to speed on derivatives trading, be careful about opening an account with them. It may be that this domicile allows them certain leeway they would not benefit from if they were headquartered somewhere else. While MF Global was regulated by some of the more sophisticated financial authorities, even here we have seen problems emerge with regulatory loopholes. Make sure you double-check that somebody responsible is keeping an eye on the company holding your cash. Nobody else is going to do it for you.

Summary: core principles of forex risk management

Most elements of effective risk management are based on common sense. I have summarised them below. Once you become more familiar with currency trading and begin managing multiple positions, or adding to existing ones, it behoves you to bring in more complex proprietary calculations to figure out your total risk. This can be hard to do, but it is an important discipline, as it allows you to make more informed trading decisions.

Risk management: the key points

1 Don't trade with money you cannot afford to lose.

2 Make sure you can cover not only your initial margin but also substantial additional margin for losing positions.

3 Make some allowance for sudden changes in margin requirement or spreads – money markets don't stand still and nor do brokers.

4 Always be aware of how much exposure you are taking on when you open a trade.

5 Always use a stop loss.

6 Be aware of how much money you could lose before your stop is hit.

7 A stop loss is not a guaranteed stop loss unless your brokerage says it is – sudden changes in the market can catch currency firms off-balance as well.

8 Consider trading with more than one company, even if it limits the amount of total margin you can take on.

9 Make sure the firm you are trading with is properly regulated.

10 Make sure you have a disaster recovery plan in place, in case you lose your internet connection or are taken ill suddenly.

4

Currencies in brief

There is a wide range of currencies available to trade and this chapter will look at most of the more commonly traded ones. They can be roughly divided into three different types:

The majors – there are really only three major globally traded currencies at the moment, and most FX traders will tend to concentrate on trading these against each other. Indeed, some traders will focus on a single currency pair only, to the exclusion of all else. The majors consist of the US dollar (USD), the euro (EUR) and the Japanese yen (JPY). The USD is the foremost, considered the reserve currency of central banks globally, and underpinning many aspects of the international financial system (e.g. most commodities are priced in US dollars, so if the dollar drops against other currencies, ergo many commodities become a bit cheaper, too).

The minor league – this is really my term for those currencies that can be traded with an FX account that are neither emerging markets currencies nor one of the majors. Most popular among these is the British pound (GBP), but other currencies that have generated interest in recent years include the Australian dollar (AUD) and the New Zealand dollar (NZD). The Swiss franc (CHF) has been a favoured defensive play in times of financial crisis and/or political uncertainty. There are also a number of other currencies, like the non-euro currencies in Europe, which regularly attract attention from traders.

Emerging markets currencies – there is increasing interest on the part of traders in some emerging markets currencies. As these economies mature and their central banks ease restrictions on their currencies, so it becomes possible to trade them. Among those that are already regularly seen on trading platforms are the likes of the Brazilian real, Eastern European currencies like the Polish zloty or the Hungarian forint, and Middle Eastern currencies such as the Israeli shekel and the Turkish lira. Bear in mind, however, that volumes in these markets are not as huge as, say, the US dollar market, so expect spreads and possibly margins to be higher in some cases, and also be aware of the potential for higher volatility.

The currency majors

The US dollar (USD)

The US dollar or 'greenback' remains the *de facto* reserve currency of the world, despite the trials and tribulations of the American economy in 2007–2011 and the downgrading of the US credit rating to AA in the summer of 2011. The US dollar has enjoyed this hallowed status since the 1940s, and while there are proposals being aired in some quarters about an alternative global reserve currency, the USD continues to be the top dog among currency traders. Eighty-five per cent of currency transactions around the world involve trades with the US dollar.

The United States is still the world's largest economy, it is the number one importer and number three exporter, and despite the fact that China has now overtaken Japan as the second largest economy, the margin between second and first place is huge.

Economic figures released by US government agencies are watched closely by currency traders. Apart from the interest rates set by the US Federal Reserve, the US central bank, other key economic statistics affecting the US dollar include Non-Farm Payrolls (NFP), the US trade balance, and various measures of consumer confidence, such as the US Consumer Confidence Index, calculated by the Conference Board.

The euro (EUR)

After the US dollar, the euro is the most widely traded foreign currency, and the EUR/USD currency pair is arguably the forex trade that sees the most activity on any given day. The euro is the latest and the most ambitious attempt at a currency union so far, and is used by 13 countries inside the European Union, with Estonia being the latest addition on 1 January 2011. It is also used outside the EU, for example as the currency of Montenegro.

The so-called Eurozone represents one of the largest and most prosperous economic blocs in the world. Interest rates for the euro are set by the European Central Bank (ECB) in Frankfurt, and are closely watched by traders. But because the Eurozone is so economically diverse, it remains difficult for currency traders to decide on the right price for the euro: economic figures released by the German government are still considered valuable, but they do not speak for the Eurozone as a whole. Increasingly, traders are focusing on data put out by the ECB and the cost of borrowing in the government bond markets for individual Eurozone governments, but even this can be an esoteric and somewhat unreliable art.

The euro was introduced onto global foreign exchange markets in 1999, three years before it became available in coins and notes. Although it suffered initially due to a lack of confidence on the part of traders and a severe downturn in the French and German economies in 2001–2003, the euro has rallied in the decade since, and was recently close to parity with sterling.

There remains a great deal of speculation in the financial media about whether the euro will be able to survive the European sovereign debt crisis, or whether the Eurozone will break up into smaller currency blocs. While some European governments such as Greece and Italy continue to struggle financially, it has been a popular currency to short against other, stronger currencies like the Canadian dollar or the Swiss franc.

Japanese yen (JPY)

The Japanese yen is one of the most popular trades in the global currency markets and is considered one of the currency 'majors'. It is the most widely traded Asian currency, even though the Chinese economy is now technically larger than Japan's. Because it is not possible to trade China's currency, the yen continues to feature high on the list of most currency traders' shopping lists.

The yen was floated as a freely tradable currency in the foreign exchange markets in 1973. In the 1970s it depreciated to around JPY300 to the US dollar. With the growth of the Japanese economy in the 1980s, the yen soared, becoming the darling of many currency traders. In 1985 it had reached 80 to the USD.

Although the Japanese economy spectacularly crashed in 1989, the yen has continued to feature in many currency trades, and the recent weakness of the euro and the US dollar has seen the yen return to levels not seen since the mid-1990s.

The Bank of Japan, the country's central bank, sets yen interest rates. Japan's base rate has remained close to zero since 1990, making it very cheap for some currency traders to borrow in yen and invest in higher-yielding assets like the New Zealand dollar (NZD), the so-called 'carry trade'.

The yen's share of global foreign exchange reserves has been trending downwards steadily since the early 1990s as banks diversify into other currencies. It reached a low of 2.9 per cent of global foreign exchange reserves in 2007 and has since increased its share at the expense of the euro and the US dollar.

The minor league

British pound (GBP)

The British pound, also widely known as sterling, is the fourth most traded currency in FX markets, after the Big Three. The pound is also favoured by central banks, which frequently keep a substantial allocation of sterling on their books.

Ever since the euro was introduced, UK governments have continued to be vexed with arguments over whether the country should join the Eurozone, but so far Britain has resisted.

The decision in 1997 by the Labour government of Tony Blair to allow the Bank of England independent powers to set UK interest rates means that the pound has become less susceptible to the sorts of politically inspired crises that have affected the currency in the past, such as the 1976 sterling crisis (when the UK was bailed out by the International Monetary Fund) or the forced withdrawal of the pound from the European Exchange Rate Mechanism (ERM) in 1992.

The pound is most frequently traded with the US dollar (the GBP/USD currency pair is often referred to as 'Cable' by FX experts on account of the transatlantic cable that was once used to communicate currency prices in the days before satellites) as well as with the euro. The European Union remains the UK's biggest trading partner, followed by the US.

The pound is regarded as a relatively responsibly managed currency at the moment, and FX investors have had a high degree of confidence in the track record of the Bank of England in managing the currency since 1997. The Bank has been tasked with keeping UK inflation rates below 2 per cent and the governor of the Bank of England must write an open letter to the Chancellor of the Exchequer (the UK finance minister) every month it fails to do so. At the time of writing, the UK inflation rate was hovering in the region of 5 per cent, well above this target, while base rates remained stubbornly low at 0.5 per cent.

More recently, the Bank has embarked on a process of 'quantitative easing' designed to help stimulate the UK economy by printing money to buy up debt. This has led to higher inflation rates, but with UK base rates so low already, it has few other options.

Swiss franc (CHF)

The Swiss franc has long been considered a currency for institutional investors to buy when they need to get out of riskier assets, particularly during times of financial crisis. Heavy buying of the Swiss franc (sometimes known as the Swissie) will happen at times of stress, when investor confidence in other assets such as shares or commodities is ebbing.

Switzerland has traditionally been regarded as a conservative and neutral country where it is safe to keep your money, hence the success of its private banking industry. Switzerland has also steered clear of EU membership and the Eurozone. It is this neutrality policy of the country's successive governments that has led its currency to be favoured by investors.

The Swiss franc was backed by gold reserves to the tune of 40 per cent, a legal requirement laid down by the Swiss government, but this was abandoned in 2000 following a referendum. In recent years it has traded very closely to the euro, maintaining a rate of approximately 1.55 to the euro. Switzerland remains heavily influenced by the economic fortunes of the Eurozone, as it is surrounded by Eurozone countries and counts the EU as its primary trading partner.

The Swiss franc will tend to rally at times of political turbulence, not just when there are financial problems. Look for it to gain strength against other major currencies when there is increasing political instability on a global scale. It is not particularly popular among central banks, and has rarely accounted for more than 0.3 per cent of global foreign exchange reserves in the past 20 years.

The Swissie is more popular with private investors than central banks, who still make use of bank accounts denominated in the currency, even though the macroeconomic case for holding Swiss francs is less powerful than it was in the late 1990s.

The Australian dollar (AUD)

The Australian dollar is one of the two major 'resource' currencies, the other being the Canadian dollar. Australia is a major producer of raw materials, particularly base metals, and as such its currency has been boosted by increasing global demand for its products. After the Japanese yen, the Australian dollar (also referred to as the 'Aussie' by currency traders) is arguably the most widely held currency in the Asia-Pacific region and is ranked number five in the world in terms of daily volume. In 2010 it accounted for 7 per cent of total global FX trading volumes.

The Aussie has been around since 1967, when Australia left the sterling area following the British pound's devaluation against the US dollar. It only became a free-trading currency in 1983, when

Australian prime minister Bob Hawke cancelled its previous peg to a basket of other currencies.

Forex traders like the AUD for a number of reasons, including Australia's exposure to the commodities price cycle, to the booming Asian economies (Australia has been a direct beneficiary of China's economic growth), and the fact that it is not one of the Big Three currencies most commonly traded. The currency tends to perform worse during bust cycles, as global demand for commodities slumps, but outperforms the more popular currencies in boom times. Australia was the first major developed nation to start raising its interest rates in the wake of the 2007–2008 crisis. Australia also never entered a technical recession during this period.

Australia has an independent central bank, the Reserve Bank of Australia, which is responsible for setting interest rates. Currency analysts and economists favour Australia because of its sound monetary policy and its political stability, as well as the AUD's correlation with resources prices.

Canadian dollar (CAD)

The Canadian dollar, also known by veteran traders as the Loonie because of the aquatic bird on the one dollar coin, is one of the two main resource-driven currencies. Like the Australian dollar, it is heavily influenced by the prices of the major commodites which Canada exports. As commodity prices go up, so often does demand for the CAD. Canada's main trading partner is the United States, so it is the USD/CAD currency pair that gets most attention from traders.

Canada's economy is heavily dependent on the raw materials the country produces, including timber, grains, base metals, gold and oil. It is also a major producer of potash, an important agricultural fertiliser. Seasoned CAD traders will follow commodities prices closely to try to gauge trends in the currency.

The Canadian dollar was first floated in 1950, although its rapid fall against the US dollar between 1960 and 1962 led to it being fixed for a period. It floated again in 1970, and parity with the USD was achieved in 1976. The CAD was cheap against the USD for much of the mid to late 1990s but came back against the greenback over the last decade, achieving parity with the USD again in 2007, and the USD fell as the US went into recession.

The CAD is held as a reserve currency by a number of central banks, particularly in the western hemisphere, where it is favoured by central banks in Latin America and the Caribbean.

Canada follows a transparent free-market system. Its interest rates are set by the Bank of Canada, the central bank, which is tasked with keeping inflation low and promoting the economic well-being of the country. The bank's governor is appointed by its directors, with the approval of the Canadian cabinet.

The Nordic currencies

Apart from the GBP and CHF, there are a number of other European currencies sitting outside the Eurozone which are frequently traded. These currencies are issued by countries which, for one reason or another, have been sceptical of the euro single-currency project and have chosen to maintain their own currencies. In addition, like Switzerland, some European countries have chosen to remain outside the European Union as well, but still constitute economies of sufficient size that traders and investors take note of their currencies.

Four Nordic countries still issue their own currencies, and these can usually be traded on most FX trading platforms.

Norwegian krone (NOK)

Norway has remained steadfastly outside the European Union. In recent history, the krone was floated by the Norwegian Central Bank (Norges Bank) in 1992 following heavy speculation against the currency by FX traders.

Although a relatively small country in terms of its population,

Norway is a major oil producer, and it is the cost of crude oil more than anything else which will tend to determine the long-term performance of the NOK against other currencies. Norway's interest rates are probably the second biggest factor.

The NOK surged in 2002 on the strength of high interest rates and a high oil price, hitting a peak at around 7.36 to the USD in July 2002. High oil prices were behind the rise of the NOK again in 2005, even as Norges Bank was cutting interest rates. When currency traders turned bearish on the USD in 2007, the NOK surged again against the dollar. Its more recent trading history has seen a steady appreciation against the greenback as traders have favoured Norway for its energy-driven economy and relatively sturdy state finances.

Swedish krona (SEK)

The Swedish krona has been floated as a currency since 1992. It has been declining against the euro since 2008 as Sweden's central bank, the Riksbank, has been cutting interest rates and has not seen fit to defend the SEK's value against the EUR, and indeed why would it, as the Eurozone accounts for a substantial share of Swedish exports. More recently, the SEK has been gaining strength, but this has more to do with the weakness of the euro than the appeal of the krona.

In 1995 Sweden signed up to join the euro but this has been hampered by political difficulties. In 2003, 56 per cent of Swedes voted against joining the euro. Since then there has been consensus in the Swedish parliament not to test the electorate again on the issue, with more recent polls demonstrating that a future euro referendum will still likely see the Swedish people voting against membership.

Such political uncertainties mean that the SEK is not regarded as a classic convergence currency, as Sweden has seemed adept at avoiding Eurozone membership so long as a substantial number of voters are opposed. No government seems prepared to risk valuable political capital on the issue, and with so many uncertainties surrounding the future of the euro itself, this situation is unlikely to change soon.

For FX traders, the popular currency to trade the SEK against is obviously the EUR.

Danish krone (DKK)

The Danish krone has been part of the ERM since 1979. It is the only currency left from the ERM II regime, which was introduced in 1999, and originally covered Denmark and Greece. When Greece joined the euro in 2001, Denmark was left on its own.

Under ERM II, the Danmarks Nationalbank keeps the DKK trading within a narrow range of plus or minus 2.25 per cent to the euro, with a benchmark rate of 7.46038 to the EUR. This means the DKK can be expected to trade broadly in line with the EUR over the long-term picture.

Officially, Denmark is meant to be joining the Eurozone at some point in the future. In 2000, the country held a referendum on Eurozone membership, but this was defeated. Since the financial crisis of 2008, Danish support for the euro has been ebbing rapidly.

What sets the DKK apart from the SEK is that euro peg, encapsulated under the ERM II regime. The Swedish central bank has no obligation to try to keep the SEK trading broadly in line with the euro. The future of ERM II and the DKK will most likely be determined by whatever new regime emerges from the current euro crisis.

So why trade the DKK against the EUR? Most FX traders tend to ignore it – unless they're Danish – but occasionally some interesting patterns can emerge for canny traders to exploit. But the big breakouts are unlikely to be there unless there was a serious attack on the Danish central bank's ability to maintain the DKK in the ERM II.

Icelandic kronur (ISK)

You will see the Icelandic kronur on some of the more advanced FX trading platforms, although it does not tend to get the attention of the NOK or the SEK. Iceland's is a small economy, and relatively poor in natural resources. Its claim to infamy was its role as one of the first economies to experience a major financial collapse in 2008, the result of its banking sector becoming overstretched.

The ISK does not see a great deal of volume, so consequently it is highly volatile, even when traded against the likes of the NOK or the SEK. In 2006, for example, the currency ranged between 50 and 80 to the USD. However, expect this lack of liquidity to also mean wider spreads in the market.

With the collapse of Iceland's banks in 2008, the government sought to peg the ISK against the EUR, but failed. The currency was officially suspended and the country was bailed out by the International Monetary Fund and others (notably Russia). In the course of 2009–2010 I saw the ISK being quoted on some trading platforms, but whether the prices quoted bore any relation to the real value of the ISK was an open question.

Local support for joining the Eurozone increased after the 2008 crisis, and the local parliament voted in 2009 to apply for EU membership.

Singapore dollar (SGD)

The Singapore Dollar was created in 1967 when the island city state became independent from neighbouring Malaysia. The SGD was originally linked to the British pound and then later the US dollar before being pegged to a secret basket of currencies. Since 1985 the currency has been floated and is free to trade via an FX account.

The Monetary Authority of Singapore (MAS) is the country's central bank and works to maintain price stability in Singapore and public confidence in the currency. The MAS uses what is called a monitoring band to maintain the rate of the SGD against those currencies it is most often exchanged against for trade purposes. These are likely to be the currencies of Singapore's main trading partners. Bear in mind that Singapore is one of the primary hubs for intra-Asian trade, and despite its small size remains a critical conduit for regional currency exchange.

Singapore's currency has not been seriously tested, unlike some other Asian currencies. During the Asian financial crisis of 1997 the MAS allowed it to depreciate by 20 per cent to help maintain Singapore's competitiveness at a time when many other regional currencies were losing value. The SGD is considered the premier currency in the Southeast Asian region and many other regional currencies can respond to sudden changes in Singapore's monetary policy. In 2010, as Singapore's economy rebounded strongly from the global recession, the MAS took the decision to allow the currency to appreciate slowly.

The SGD is a good currency to watch for traders interested in the progress of Asian economies and trade. While not as liquid as, say, the JPY, it is prone to sudden bounces if the MAS makes any announcements regarding its management of the currency.

Hong Kong dollar (HKD)

The Hong Kong dollar has been pegged to the US dollar since 1972. Prior to this, it had been linked to the British pound. Hong Kong maintained the US currency peg until 1983, when a new regime was introduced that allowed banks to exchange HKD for USD at a fixed rate while a floating rate was maintained for other transactions (e.g. changing money at an airport). However, the existence of a fixed rate within the banking system has meant that there is little difference between the bank rate and the USD/HKD rate.

The fact that HKD is available to trade at all on FX platforms reflects the growing importance of the Chinese customer base for brokerages more than anything else. It is also ranked eighth globally in terms of global foreign exchange market turnover. Some local traders prefer to trade HKD as their base currency rather than USD. In addition, with the absence of a floated currency for mainland China, the HKD is the only real substitute.

There are also intra-day possibilities for the trader of HKD. Many traders at the time of writing were focused on the possibility that the Hong Kong Monetary Authority would switch its peg to the Chinese

yuan to better reflect realities in the local economy (low unemployment and a property bubble). This might also involve a one-off 30 per
cent revaluation of the HKD against the USD as an interim measure.
Long-term strategies of this kind – trying to second guess Hong Kong
monetary policy – can be better managed using options rather than
other types of FX trading account.

New Zealand dollar (NZD)

Despite its relatively small share of global GDP, New Zealand's currency is still in the top 10 in terms of daily FX volume. Called the
Kiwi by FX traders (after the diminutive local flightless bird of the
same name), it was one half of the famous 'carry trade' in the last
decade, which saw many investors borrow JPY at low rates to buy
high-yielding NZD.

The NZD's value was determined by a trade-weighted basket of currencies from 1973 to 1985, before the currency was floated. It remains
a fairly volatile currency: because there are fewer New Zealand dollars
in circulation than the other top 10 currencies, speculators can move
the price around. Higher prevailing interest rates in New Zealand
have also led some investors to buy the Kiwi. This has forced New
Zealand's central bank to intervene on at least three occasions in the
last decade, selling currency in order to try to force down the NZD. It
has met with mixed success.

What is XAU/XAG?

You will sometimes see XAU or XAG quoted as part of a currency pair
on some forex trading platforms. XAU is gold quoted as a currency
and XAG is silver. These currency pairs, for example XAU/USD, let
you trade a currency against gold or silver. Hundreds of years ago
they were used as a currency themselves, and within living memory
currencies were still linked to the gold price. The US left the gold
standard (which allowed for US dollars to be converted into the
equivalent value in gold held by the Federal Reserve) only in 1971,

and as recently as 2000 40 per cent of Swiss francs in circulation were backed by gold.

So why trade a currency pair like XAU/USD (see Figure 4.1)? There has been increased interest in trading gold against currencies in the last 18 months as the gold price has strengthened. Precious metals, because of their historical status as stores of value and currencies in themselves, have gained in value against paper currencies as central banks have printed more money to facilitate quantitative easing. Traders and central banks know there is only a finite supply of precious metals out there in the world – the mining industry can only dig up and refine a small amount of gold every year. Central banks can't print gold. In addition, gold is not subject to the same inflationary pressures as paper money.

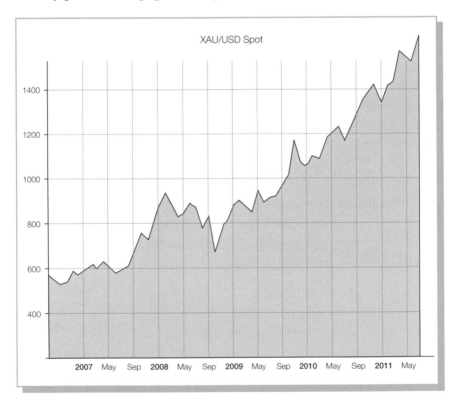

© ProRealTime.com

Figure 4.1 XAU/USD 2007–2011

This has led to a situation where some FX traders have wanted to trade gold against the US dollar in particular. They have wanted to exploit what they see as a strong trend of declining dollars and rising gold prices.

What to trade

When getting started in forex trading, it is best to trade one of the major currency pairs, and some FX traders never go beyond this. They find they get all the price action they need in these highly liquid markets.

The most popular currency markets are EUR/USD and GBP/USD. After that USD/JPY is frequently traded, along with the so-called resource currencies, AUD, CAD and NZD. Most traders like to keep the USD on one side of the trade because it is the global reserve currency and a benchmark for many FX traders and analysts.

Once you become more experienced, you may want to branch out into other markets. For example, you might seek out particular developing trends based on technical analysis, and this may lead you to markets where there is no USD component – GBP/JPY, for instance. Or you may want to strip out your USD exposure completely. Some currency markets can end up range-bound for quite some time, leaving the experienced FX trader with little scope to make money.

Ultimately, much will depend on your style of trading, your personal psychology and your risk tolerance.

5

Trading emerging markets currencies

Some forex trading platforms now provide access to emerging markets currencies. There is a wide variety of emerging markets currencies available, including Czech koruna (CZK), Polish zloty (PLN), Turkish lira (TRY), Israeli shekel (ISK), South African rand (ZAR) and even the Brazilian real (BRL). A currency will generally be made available to FX traders if there is enough demand and enough liquidity in the underlying interbank market. It also has to be free to trade. Some currencies, notably China's yuan, are still not freely available and unlikely to be any time soon. China protects its currency jealously, and the yuan's relative cheapness versus the US dollar has become something of a political hot potato between Beijing and Washington DC in recent years.

Emerging markets currencies tend to come in and out of favour with traders, although at the time of writing, volumes in emerging markets currencies were picking up, with some brokers adding more esoteric currencies to their platforms. Part of this is down to the solid performance of some emerging economies during 2009–2011, which led to a demand from traders wanting to benefit from the gradual appreciation of some currencies. For example, the Polish economy was one of the few European economies to perform well in the immediate aftermath of the credit crisis, and this led to some speculative activity on the long side of the Polish zloty.

Traders also like 'fringe' European currencies because they hope that one day they will join the Eurozone – being judged suitable for Eurozone membership is a major stamp of approval for FX traders and other investors.

Although the Polish government has said it hopes to join the Eurozone in 2012, the problems surrounding Greece and the future of the euro bloc mean choppy times ahead for the zloty and other European currencies with Eurozone ambitions.

Traders approaching emerging markets currencies need to bear in mind a number of factors:

■ Most emerging markets currencies will trade against the USD, although there are some more esoteric pairs out there. It makes sense, for example, for a broker to offer EUR/PLN because of the currency convergence play involved, and I've even seen PLN/JPY on one trading platform, although there was very little volume in it.

■ Emerging markets currencies tend to be more thinly traded than the big 10 currencies. They are often still tightly controlled by their central bank, even though they have been floated. Because volumes in the interbank market are thinner, this means a central bank can have more of an impact if it starts selling or buying its own currency. This can lead to more volatility spikes against a high-volume currency like USD.

■ Brokers may require higher margins and/or quote wider spreads on emerging markets currencies. This is simply being passed on from the interbank market, where trade will also be thinner. If you are planning to trade large amounts in these markets, be aware that trades may not be as quick to go through, particularly in the spot FX market.

■ Many emerging markets protect their currencies by linking them to a trade-weighted basket of currencies, usually comprised of the currencies of their major trading partners. The central bank will seek to keep the currency trading within a certain relationship to that basket, buying and selling either covertly or overtly as the need arises. Because the currencies can be thinly traded, this is easier to do.

■ As emerging economies become increasingly important, so do their currencies. Overall, many commentators expect them to continue to gain ground against some of the more established currencies, creating some good medium- to long-term trends for the trader.

As you can see from comparing Figures 5.1 and 5.2 the sheer volume of trades being transacted in EUR/USD provides for a much smoother trend if you were looking to bet against the euro than EUR/PLN. The zloty is much, much more volatile and prone to sudden moves. But, on the other side of the coin, you can benefit from some big price moves, as in the second half of 2008, when investors were exiting the zloty at high speed. Because there were fewer participants in the market, the big sell-off in emerging markets assets as the credit crunch took hold had a major impact on the zloty, producing a big price swing for those long the euro against the Polish currency.

When trading emerging markets currencies, be aware that you may have to pay for a higher rate of margin and see wider spreads than you might be used to with the EUR or USD. This is because there is simply less of that currency being traded globally – there are far fewer zlotys in circulation than US dollars. Emerging markets currencies can also be more volatile than the majors, with sudden changes in price, so be sure you protect yourself with stop losses.

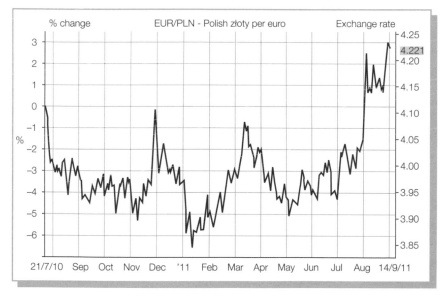

www.alphaterminal.co.uk
© Ionic Information Ltd

Figure 5.1　EUR/PLN 2010–2011

www.alphaterminal.co.uk
© Ionic Information Ltd

Figure 5.2   EUR/USD 2007–2011

The appeal of trading emerging markets

As I've already mentioned, some emerging markets currencies had a good run against the USD during the recent liquidity crisis.

The increased volatility inherent in emerging markets currencies makes them attractive to the short-term trader. Take, for example, the South African rand in a typical week, as illustrated in Figure 5.3. As you can see, FX traders who are able to set their stops sufficiently wide to take account of the intra-day fluctuations which you will see in a currency like the rand will also be able to capitalise on substantial volatility.

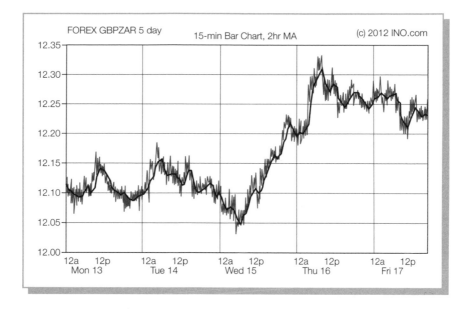

© ProRealTime.com

Figure 5.3   The South African rand – a typical week

Leading emerging markets currencies

Brazilian real (BRL)

The Brazilian real is starting to find its way onto FX trading platforms as Brazil becomes a more important component of the global
economy, and it continues to appreciate against the US dollar, despite
the best efforts of the Brazilian government to rein it in. Not all
brokers offer the BRL, but expect to see it become prevalent in the
near future.

The current iteration of the real came into being in 1994, as part of the government's financial modernisation plan (Plano Real), intended to put an end to 30 years of inflation. It is really the first of the Latin American currencies to be traded on a wider scale by retail traders – many others are simply not floated or are pegged to the US dollar.

Even the real was at one stage pegged to the USD on a 1:1 basis. Since it has floated it dropped to as low as four to the USD, although in recent years it has been appreciating steadily, despite the efforts of the central bank and the government to rein it in. Central bank meddling contributed in a fall in the real towards the end of 2011, along with a tax on the purchase of Brazilian bonds by foreigners.

Brazil is going to be the most important economy in Latin America for some time to come and it is also a major exporter of some important global commodities, particularly sugar, ethanol, soybeans and coffee. Consequently, the real can sometimes be influenced by commodities prices.

Israeli shekel (ISK)

One of the few free-floating currencies in the Middle East, the Israeli shekel has been steadily gaining ground on the USD in the last 10 years. It became free to trade in the forex market in 2003, and shekel futures were launched on the Chicago Mercantile Exchange in 2007.

The Israeli economy has been expanding into industry and high technology, diversifying away from stalwarts such as tourism, agriculture and the defence business. Interest in trading the ISK has been growing, and you will now see it quoted by many FX dealers.

Because volumes in the ISK are thinner than in some other currencies, fears are rife that foreign investors will try to make a fast buck by speculating on the shekel market, and indeed there is often a fair amount of 'hot' speculative money in this currency. Investors need to be particularly aware of its potential volatility.

The debate continues in Israeli financial circles as to whether having a free-floating currency is really a good thing.

South African rand (ZAR)

Currently the only African currency you are likely to see quoted by your broker, the ZAR is heavily influenced by the prices of some of the resources mined in South Africa, particularly gold and platinum. Expect it to react and indeed to correlate to moves in the gold price. Some traders like to try to arbitrage between the price of gold and the ZAR.

The ZAR has been gradually losing ground to the USD since the early 1980s. A worsening current account deficit, problems with the labour market, political corruption, and an aversion on the part of some investors to emerging markets post-2008 has continued to punish it. Problems with the country's electricity utilities, particularly Eskom, and power shortages that have caused temporary shutdowns of important mines, mean the ZAR has been suffering from volatility.

On the one hand, a higher gold price is pushing the rand up against developed world currencies, but on the other any piece of negative news coming out of South Africa will tend to drive it down.

Turkish lira (TRY)

Once branded the world's least valuable currency, the Turkish lira had to have six zeroes knocked off and be reconstituted in order to bring it back into line with other currencies. Thirty years of chronic inflation in Turkey had led to a situation where the country was minting lira coins in denominations of 250,000 at the end of the last century.

Since 2005 the TRY has been benefiting from Turkey's vibrant economy, and while EU membership remains a distant dream, it is one of the few Middle Eastern currencies in which traders can freely speculate. Another attractive factor has been the relatively high interest rates (double digits) that have been prevailing in Turkey. This has led to a 'carry trade' situation where investors borrow in low-interest currencies like USD or GBP to buy TRY. With some Turkish banks paying interest as high as 12 per cent this still allows investors to make a considerable profit if they have the credit lines.

In 2009 the Chicago Mercantile Exchange added Turkish lira futures to its emerging markets currencies contracts, again on the back of increasing interest from traders in Turkey and emerging markets generally. The currency remains fairly volatile, and traders participating in this market will need deep pockets if they are to set their stops widely enough.

As with some other emerging markets currencies, the TRY tends to fluctuate in line with investor appetite for emerging markets investments: when investors are feeling more aggressive, they will be buying Turkish assets and hence will need lira; as soon as they start to take fright, they will be selling lira again. Traders of the TRY will need to be acutely aware of where the market 'noise' is in this respect.

Polish zloty (PLN)

Can Poland still be classified as an emerging market? It is one of those swiftly modernising countries on the cusp of being fully recognised as a developed market. Already a member of the EU, it is also technically obliged to join the Eurozone at some point, although it has not specified when, and recent problems with the euro bloc may have pushed its entry date further into the future.

Poland's current currency, the zloty, remains one of those convergence currencies which traders believe is living on borrowed time. Because there is this belief that eventually the PLN will be dropped in favour of the EUR, the market tries to push it up against the EUR. The primary currency pairs to trade, therefore, are the benchmark USD/PLN, and EUR/PLN although strangely I have also seen PLN/JPY on one trading platform (this may have been a 'carry trade' play, based on Japan's low interest rates versus Poland's).

The PLN is the most heavily traded and most liquid of the Eastern European currencies. It can be affected, sometimes somewhat irrationally, by regional financial problems, for example in Hungary, or when some Eurozone banks were off-loading assets in Eastern Europe in 2009 because of credit problems. Poland does, however, have a larger and generally more prosperous economy than many of its Eastern European neighbours and is able to weather economic storms more readily than they are.

Hungarian forint (HUF)

Another former Warsaw Pact member now in the EU, and theoretically destined to join the Eurozone at some point, is Hungary. Unlike Poland (above), Hungary's recent financial history is more problematic. The country's currency, the Hungarian forint, is regularly punished by FX traders whenever it looks as though it is flirting with a default.

Hungary's financial and political scene never seems to stand still, and any negative news coming out of Budapest will see the HUF take a hammering. It is a very volatile currency, and responsible for my worst ever trade in emerging markets currencies! A good example of this volatility is the fact that in 2009 it was one of the best performing currencies in the world, on the back of the carry trade into the HUF. Despite losing half its value against the USD in 2008, and flirting with a debt default in 2009, high interest rates in Hungary led to many investors buying the HUF to benefit from the potentially high yield.

Fast forward to the end of 2011 and we have the forint hitting a record low against the EUR on the back of fears that it was going to default. This demonstrates just how swiftly sentiment in the HUF can change. It is almost a Jekyll and Hyde scenario – one moment the darling of FX traders, the next moment a villain. It is a good currency if you have the appetite for trading a highly volatile currency subject to wide swings, less good for the conservative trend follower.

The HUF has been fully convertible and fully tradable with other currencies since 2001, with EUR/HUF being one of the obvious trades.

Czech koruna (CZK)

The Czech koruna is the third of the big Eastern European currencies you are likely to encounter on an FX trading platform. It was introduced in 1993 when the Czech Republic and Slovakia decided to go their own ways. It is also the most thinly traded out of the CZK, PLN and HUF.

Technically, the Czechs were meant to join the euro in 2012, but the government abandoned this plan in 2007. While Eurozone membership is still meant to happen at some time in the future, only about 20 per cent of Czechs currently support the idea, and the ongoing negative news flow coming from inside the Eurozone is unlikely to change the minds of the majority.

Traditionally, the CZK was considered something of a regional safe haven for those trading European currencies. Investors would buy CZK when there was trouble brewing next door in Hungary, for example. However, the Czech Republic is also highly dependent on its trade and commercial ties with the Eurozone, particularly Germany, and problems with the euro have also had a knock-on effect on the CZK.

The fact that the Czech Republic is highly dependent on its exports, particularly to neighbouring Eurozone countries, has not helped the CZK. While its finances may be healthier than those of some of its neighbours, and its political culture more stable and less prone to extremes of corruption, the health of Czech export markets will always be important for the CZK.

Emerging markets currency trading tips

1 Be prepared for volatility: this means making sure your stops are set very wide. These markets tend to be the preserve of wealthier traders who can take big hits if they get it wrong. They are not kind to traders seeking predictable trends stretching over several months.

2 Most emerging markets currency trades are against the USD, although European currencies are also heavily traded against the EUR.

3 Trade is thinner in these currencies, causing frequent bouts of volatility.

4 The carry trade is often a big motivating factor, prompting enthusiasm for a currency if there is a big interest rate difference versus the relatively low rates prevailing in developed countries at the time of writing.

5 Traders will often sell one of these currencies on rumours of sovereign debt problems: just the sight of an International Monetary Fund executive in a hotel lobby in Budapest is enough to set them off.

6 Sometimes markets suffer from guilt by association: in 1995, during the infamous peso crisis in Latin America, traders also sold the Philippine peso for no other real reason than its name. Such moves can be short term in nature, but still significant.

7 Expect spreads to be wider for emerging markets currencies, and watch out for liquidity problems if you are trading with bigger sums, particularly during a quiet period in the market.

8 If a country is a big exporter of natural resources, it is worth keeping an eye on how those commodities are performing. Watch out for arbitrage opportunities and educate yourself about that particular commodity's price cycle. No trader of the ZAR should be ignorant of what is happening in the gold market.

9 Emerging markets are more of a trade-the-news game than G10 currencies. Technical analysis still works, but because there are fewer traders watching these markets on a full-time basis, it is less effective as a predictor of future price moves.

10 Emerging markets investments do well when the market overall is in search of riskier assets: when investors become fearful, their emerging markets assets are often the first to be sold off. This will tend to push the currency they are denominated in downwards. When the market is not able to make up its mind as to whether it wants risk or not, these currencies will bounce around.

11 Politics remains an important factor in emerging markets: if you are planning on following a currency for more than three months, make sure you study the political situation. A rabble-rousing speech by a British member of parliament may not move the GBP, but it could affect the HUF if reported widely enough.

6

What moves the markets?

There is a range of what we call macroeconomic factors that can have a big impact on currency prices. While some traders pay more attention to these than others, it is useful for anybody opening an FX trading account to have at least some idea of what it is that moves currency markets. It will at least help you to interpret what some of the analysts are talking about, as well as to get a feel for what the market is thinking about.

Central banks

Central banks are very important players in the currency markets. They are often responsible for printing actual physical bank notes, but they also need to manage the supply of that currency in the global economy. Too much in circulation could mean inflation – the currency becomes worth less. Too little, and the country or currency bloc could face the prospect of recession, for example. It is a delicate balancing act to maintain.

Each central bank has its own mandate or objectives that it is seeking to achieve, and it will try to execute this policy through a variety of economic tools it has at its disposal. The goals of central banks are broadly similar, although not identical. In addition, they reach their decisions through different organisational structures.

Below we look at the central banks that currency traders follow most closely, and you will hear them discussed on a regular basis by forex analysts.

US Federal Reserve

The Federal Reserve, most often referred to simply as the Fed, is the US central bank. With the US dollar still acting as the *de facto* reserve currency for the global economy and other central banks, FX traders will focus on the pronouncements of the Federal Reserve to a much larger degree. The Fed was created in 1913 and today pursues the goal of maximum employment in the US, stable prices and moderate long-term interest rates. It also has a brief to maintain financial stability within the US markets. Management of US monetary policy is carried out by a board of governors, led by the chairman of the Federal Reserve, as well as by the Federal Open Market Committee (FOMC), which consists of the board of the Fed, the president of the Federal Reserve Bank of New York, and the presidents of four of the other US regional reserve banks who serve on a rotating basis. The Fed does not issue US federal debt (Treasury bonds): that is the job of the US Treasury, which manages America's national debt. However, the Fed can buy and sell Treasuries as part of its quantitative easing processes.

European Central Bank

With the creation of the euro there was also a need for some kind of central bank to authorise the issue of currency and to keep inflation under control within the Eurozone. The ECB sets the interest rates for the Eurozone but is not responsible for issuing or managing the debt of the various countries within the currency bloc. It is constituted as a corporation, with the various European Union central banks acting as shareholders. At the time of writing, the ECB targets price stability at around 2 per cent over the medium term. Since 2010 the role of the ECB has been expanded, with the creation of the European Financial Stability Facility to provide loans to countries and financial institutions in difficulty. It has also been more active as a buyer of the debt of member nations in an effort to avoid a default. Because of the importance of the euro to the global economy, FX traders pay particular attention to the pronouncements of the governor of the ECB.

Bank of Japan

Japan founded its own central bank following the Meiji Restoration in 1868 and it has been largely responsible for Japanese monetary policy since the yen was floated in the early 1970s. The BoJ used to impose credit growth quotas on Japanese banks – i.e. it sought to control the amount of lending going on in the Japanese economy by authorising bank lending – but this helped to create the infamous Japanese bubble economy which consigned the country to the doldrums for the 1990s and beyond. The BoJ has a range of responsibilities, but most importantly it sets interest rates (although yen rates have remained steadfastly low ever since I've been working as a financial writer). More recently the BoJ has acted to intervene in global currency markets in order to prevent the yen from becoming too expensive: FX traders are now aware that there is a point at which the BoJ will sell yen into the market to keep it from becoming too expensive. This is particularly important for Japan, as it is still very much an export-driven economy and its manufacturers don't want to see their products becoming too expensive.

Bank of England

After Sweden's central bank, the Bank of England is the oldest central bank in the world, having been founded in 1694. Since 1998 it has been responsible for managing the pound sterling, as well as setting UK interest rates. Monetary policy is set by the bank's Monetary Policy Committee (MPC), chaired by the governor. In the wake of the 2008 financial crisis, the bank has also been taking on more responsibility for regulating banks. The bank's primary objective is monetary stability, i.e. keeping the UK inflation rate below 2 per cent. This has become more difficult in recent history, as global commodities prices coupled with a policy of quantitative easing have driven up inflation in the UK. The bank does not manage the issuance of UK sovereign debt – this is now handled by the UK Debt Management Office, which assumed the role in 1998. The MPC publishes the minutes of its rate-setting deliberations two weeks after its meetings. These are picked over in detail by analysts and traders interested in trading the GBP.

Swiss National Bank

The Swiss franc (CHF) or Swissie remains an important safe haven currency for traders and other investors, and typically will rise in value during periods of financial instability.

The Swiss National Bank is Switzerland's central bank, tasked with maintaining price stability in Switzerland and building an appropriate environment for economic growth. Its decisions can have a major impact on the performance of the Swiss franc. Monetary policy decisions are based on a medium term inflation forecast, which is an important barometer for forex traders seeking to predict how the SNB will act.

The SNB conducts an in-depth monetary policy assessment in March, June, September and December. It uses the three month Libor market for CHF to steer interest rate levels. Under Switzerland's National Bank Act, the SNB also works to contribute to stability in Switzerland's financial markets.

The bank intervened in the USD/CHF market in 2011 as the Swiss currency was steadily appreciating, partly due to flight out of the EUR. The wife of the then-governor of the SNB controversially placed a profitable forex trade with Bank Sarasin shortly before the intervention occurred, leading to political scandal in Switzerland and the eventual resignation of her husband.

The SNB has been seeking to maintain a cap at around 1.20 CHF to the EUR in an effort to protect the currency from appreciating against the EUR. This has been in place since September 2011.

For FX traders, central banks are important for a number of reasons:

1 They set interest rates (see below). This will dictate the cost of borrowing and lending in a given currency. In recent history, interest rates have tended not to change much – usually no more than 0.25 per cent (25 basis points) at a time – but the time may come one day when this will change again. Central banks seem to be better at managing rates than politicians were.

2 They have an excellent insight into how the local economy is doing. Traders will focus on what central bank governors say when they announce whether rates are changing or not. The conventional view is that they might give away some clues as to the real state of the economy and the direction of future monetary policy.

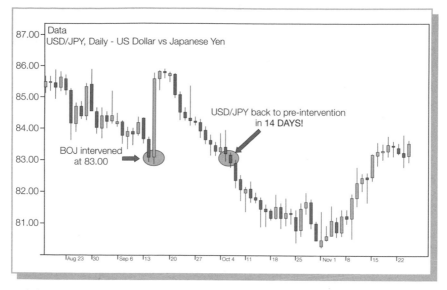

Source: www.babypips.com

Figure 6.1   Effect of Bank of Japan's intervention on USD/JPY

3 They can intervene directly in financial markets. This can substantially move a currency, creating either massive profits if you're on the right side of the trade, or big losses if you are on the wrong side and with no stop loss in place. Currency interventions are unpredictable: banks don't like to tell the market they're going to intervene before it happens, as this makes the whole exercise more costly for them. The element of surprise is critical. Figure 6.1 illustrates how the yen moved suddenly against the USD when the Bank of Japan intervened.

4 Central banks manage a country's foreign currency reserves, which can often be very substantial. Most central banks, for example, own large quantities of USD, making it the world's *de facto* reserve currency. But recent erosion of global confidence in the Eurozone, for example, has led some central banks to sell their EUR, helping to push this currency down. Central banks don't often advertise their foreign currency operations, but consistent buying or selling by G20 central banks can have a substantial impact.

Interest rates

Central banks frequently set base rates as part of their political mandate. Rates will impact the cost of borrowing and lending a currency. They are one of the tools central banks use to help them to curb inflation. A low interest rate – for example, that charged for JPY over the last couple of decades – will often mean investors will borrow that currency to buy others, the so-called 'carry trade'.

However, higher rates also mean investors are being encouraged to put money on deposit, thereby taking money out of circulation and calming inflationary pressure. Banks and mortgage providers tend to react in line with official central bank rates, raising or lowering their own rates accordingly. This also means that there is less currency in circulation, which can make it more expensive relative to other currencies. This is never a good idea for countries that rely heavily on churning out exports.

Take New Zealand as an example. The country's economy is relatively small, which means there is generally less NZD in circulation than,

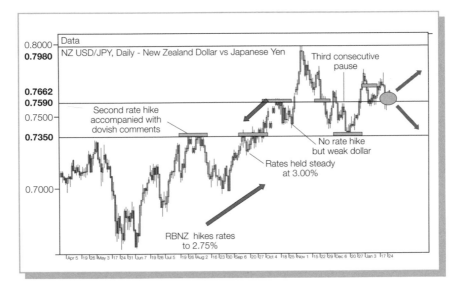

Source: www.babypips.com

Figure 6.2   USD/NZD: impact of interest rate changes

say, USD. However, New Zealand also accounts for an enormous proportion of the cross-border dairy industry – approximately 30 per cent of the total volume of dairy products exported globally. This means that New Zealand's central bank needs to make sure the NZD does not climb too high against the USD. In 2008 New Zealand's base rate was 8.25 per cent, extremely high when compared with the base rates in the G10 countries at this time, making it a 'hot' currency for investors. The Reserve Bank of New Zealand cut rates in an effort to keep the NZD competitive against the currencies of major markets, like the US.

In Figure 6.2 you can see the dramatic impact on the NZD/USD currency pair from a rise in interest rates by the Royal Bank of New Zealand. It is also interesting to note that while New Zealand's central bank raises the rate again later in the summer, the 'dovish' comments issued at the same time mean that there is no precipitate buying of the NZD by traders. Later in the year, it is the weaker USD rather than a strong NZD that becomes the more 'active' side of the trade. The central bank is sitting out for the time being.

Higher interest rates are not the be-all and end-all for FX markets – they can't save a currency if the country's economy and balance

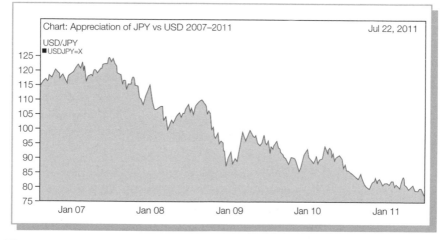

Source: Yahoo!

Figure 6.3   Appreciation of JPY vs USD 2007–2011

sheet have other fundamental problems – but changes in base rates can cause temporary spikes in FX markets, particularly if the market as a whole is not expecting them. Take Japan, where the economy has been struggling since the end of the 'bubble' market that country experienced in the 1980s. While the Bank of Japan has kept rates steadfastly low, and the equities market has struggled, the JPY has been getting steadily stronger against the USD over the last few years (see Figure 6.3).

Economic growth

Arguably of more importance than base rates is the overall rate of economic growth that an economy experiences. These figures are usually released on a quarterly basis and often come out as an estimate in advance of real numbers that are often revised upwards or downwards. It is, however, the initial estimate that FX traders tend to focus on – by the time revised figures come out, their attention has often moved elsewhere. In different countries, different government agencies are responsible for collating the data used to assess how well an economy is doing. Solid economic growth is a strong positive for the currency concerned, while weak growth or even a recession (economic contraction over two consecutive quarters) will bode ill for a currency.

It is because of strong economic growth being experienced in countries like Brazil and Turkey that there is more interest now in the performance of emerging markets currencies. It is likely that volumes in currencies like the Brazilian real will pick up over the next few years as Brazil's economy continues to expand.

While government forecasts are considered important, FX traders often consider the independent views of investment banks, which also release macroeconomic forecasts.

Unemployment

Higher unemployment is an indicator of an economy that is strug-gling. Jobless rates are regularly released by governments, and FX traders will be looking to see whether they have increased or decreased against the previous month or quarter. Analysts will be aware of whether there are seasonal adjustments that also need to be applied, as jobless rates in a country can fluctuate regularly.

The most important employment indicator for FX traders is the US Non-Farm Payroll figure, which comes out on the first Friday of the month. This will show how the US employment rate has changed over the past month or so, and is quoted in increments of 10,000. It does not include farming jobs, as the agricultural industry is more seasonal in nature and still important enough in the US to affect the employment picture on a regular basis (and thus obscure the real health of the underlying economy).

The US jobless rate, also published by the US Labor Department, is another key unemployment indicator. If it remains consistently below 375,000 on a week-to-week basis, economists believe that this shows a long-term improvement trend in the underlying economy.

Adjustments to unemployment are important to investors, including FX traders, because they are a leading economic indi-cator. This means that it can provide advance warning of an improving economic situation for the country and currency con-cerned. Unemployment has been followed particularly closely by the market in recent years as traders have sought signs of an improving global economic situation, and some signs that the US is pulling out of the doldrums.

Inflation

Inflation is of particular interest to FX traders as ultimately it affects the medium-term value of currency. By 'printing' money, for example through the process known as quantitative easing, which has been in vogue among central banks in recent years, central banks are increasing the amount of currency in circulation. This fuels inflation and will weaken a currency against those of trade partners.

High rates of inflation – over 2–3 per cent – can start to be bad news for any economy. It will also lead traders to sell that currency against others, as it is expected that it will become increasingly cheap. Central banks will try to curb inflation by raising interest rates, but it can be a delicate balancing act.

Depending on the country, inflation figures are calculated slightly differently and reported differently. Most major economies will publish a Consumer Price Index (CPI) and a Retail Price Index (RPI). The CPI, often called the 'headline inflation rate', measures the increase – or decrease – in a typical basket of consumer goods. It is the price of items that the average consumer will commonly need to buy, including the likes of transport and medical care (if this needs to be paid for). The RPI tends not to include the cost of housing – mortgage rates, for example. Most traders and analysts will focus on the CPI, which is commonly used in the US and by the European Commission.

In the US, the Bureau of Labor Statistics is responsible for compiling and publishing inflation numbers. It produces a number of different indicators, most of which will be mulled over by analysts and FX traders. The headline rate is CPI For All Urban Consumers. Food and energy inflation are also tracked separately, as are gasoline and household energy. This allows investors and analysts to strip out the impact on overall inflation of commodities markets such as oil and gas.

A ready source of information on inflation in the European Union and the Eurozone is Eurostat, which publishes much of the economic data compiled by the European Commission. It produces inflation figures for the wider EU area, as well as for the Eurozone. It also breaks these down into rates for individual European economies. It even compiles sub-indices, measuring the likes of inflation in food, alcohol and tobacco, and clothing.

In Japan, the CPI and the RPI are calculated and broadcast by the Ministry of Internal Affairs and Communication.

Business and consumer confidence

Traders like to have an idea of how confident business leaders and ordinary consumers are in a given country. Indexes which track business and consumer confidence are usually compiled independently, i.e. not by government departments, and are based on regular survey data. These indicators tend to be looked at more closely by investors in shares rather than currencies, but FX traders often like to use them as an additional measure when trying to assess the direction of a particular currency.

Purchasing Managers Index (PMI) – many industrialised countries conduct surveys of purchasing managers in both the manufacturing and services sectors. This can be seen as a measure of whether an economy is contracting or expanding. There are various PMIs that are popular with traders: for example, the Markit Eurozone Manufacturing PMI is closely followed by traders interested in the euro, while those with CAD exposure might look to the RBC Canadian Manufacturing PMI. In the US, the PMI has been compiled by the Institute of Supply Management (ISM) since 1948. Outside the US, it tends to be conducted by Markit. A rating of 42–50 is usually seen as good news, indicating that the economy or the business sector under review is expanding. However, traders and analysts also focus on month-to-month changes: if a PMI is declining from, say, 52 one month to 48 the next, that is not good news.

Tankan Survey – conducted by the Bank of Japan, this is a survey of major Japanese businesses published four times a year. It polls companies on trends and conditions and on their planned spending. It is seen by some traders as a sound measure of the direction of the Japanese economy, and more specifically the Japanese yen.

ZEW Index – this is a survey conducted in Germany of 350 financial experts. It measures how many of them are optimistic versus pessimistic about the future of the German economy over the next six months. Because of the importance of the German economy to the Eurozone, it is still studied by some currency traders as an underlying indicator for the euro. It is expressed as the difference between those experts who are positive and those who are negative. Thus, if 40 per cent are positive and 30 per cent are negative, the ZEW would be +10 per cent. Those pundits who think the economy will remain relatively neutral are not counted.

Consumer Confidence – Polls of consumer confidence are a useful measure of how much money consumers are likely to spend, and how much money they are likely to be pumping into the economy and into circulation. In the US, the Conference Board bases the US Consumer Confidence Index on a monthly survey of 5,000 households. This is also followed closely by the US Federal Reserve and influences its monetary policy.

Foreign trade

Trade flows are often assessed by traders because they will show how much demand there is likely to be for a country's currency. If more people are buying goods and resources from a country, there will be demand for its currency. If there is a net trade deficit – the country is importing more than it is exporting – the impact is going to be negative, as there is much more selling going on.

Trade figures are not the be-all and end-all for the forex trader, but they can be important for export-driven economies or those with large natural resources sectors like Australia or Canada.

The current account balance is a key measure of a country's foreign trade, as it shows how much foreign exchange it is holding. If a country has a current account deficit it means its foreign currency reserves are going down, making it harder for firms to buy foreign currency and trade internationally. A current account surplus takes some pressure off the central bank, allowing it more scope to shape monetary policy, while a deficit will leave it more at the mercy of other, stronger currencies.

If the current account deficit increases consistently, this could lead investors to dump the currency as its value is eroded. For traders, this could produce a solid trend, giving them the opportunity to short the currency.

National/sovereign debt

This is the amount of money governments borrow, usually via the global bond markets. The securities issued by governments when they borrow are called by a number of names: Bunds in Germany, Treasuries in the US, gilts in the UK. The amount of money a government borrows in the bond markets, and how much it borrows (and spends) versus how much it makes from taxes, can also impact its currency. Why?

In recent years we have seen borrowing by some EU countries reach a point where it has begun to have a negative effect on the euro. This is because investors fear that either these countries will default on their debts or the Eurozone itself will be broken up. It creates fear and uncertainty in the market, and leads to investors off-loading euro in favour of other currencies like CHF or GBP. Among the figures traders will focus on is the degree of take-up of debt in auctions and the relative enthusiasm of investors for a country's debt.

A default – when a country can no longer meet its debt obligations – will have a negative impact on its currency and can have severe knock-on impacts on other major trading partners. Until recently, this was not a consideration for currency majors and tended to affect only emerging markets currencies. However, the prospect of a default by one or more members of the Eurozone and the high level of borrowing by several countries within this bloc has had a major impact on the euro.

Natural disasters and conflict

Natural disasters and military conflicts or revolutions can have a substantial impact on even major currencies, but more particularly on the fortunes of emerging market currencies. However, if a country is hit by a natural disaster this does not necessarily mean its currency will be sold. In March 2011, when Japan was hit by an earthquake and a tsunami, and thousands of people died, many traders took this as a negative signal and sold the JPY. However, the currency quickly rallied as Japanese insurance companies sold foreign assets and bought yen in order to meet claims. This is what happened following the lesser Kobe quake in 1995 as well, so there was historical precedent (see Figure 6.4). Note how a major uptrend is followed by a steady decline – the USD/JPY is seeking its equilibrium again.

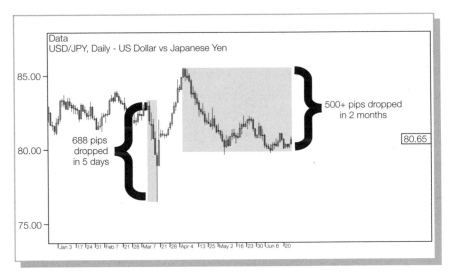

Source: www.babypips.com

Figure 6.4   Volatility in the yen caused by the March 2011 earthquake and tsunami

Commodities prices

Many commodities – although not all – are denominated in US dollars. This is largely because the benchmark futures contracts for these commodities are traded in Chicago or New York. Because of this, changes in the price of the USD can also affect the price of commodities. Arguably of most importance to the FX trader is the price of gold, as this is often regarded as a currency in its own right (the gold supply is limited by the amount of gold mined, and there is not that much of it). Gold is a good indicator of confidence in FX markets: traders will buy gold if they fear inflation or lack confidence in other financial markets. Beyond gold, however, natural resources prices can also impact the currencies of countries which are big exporters, like Australia and Canada (see Figure 6.5).

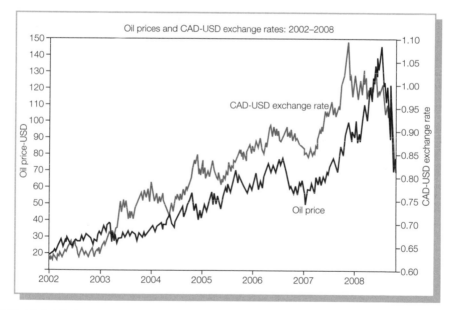

Source: The Armchair Trader

Figure 6.5   CAD/USD correlation with crude oil

Other important economic indicators

Housing starts

Since 2008 there has been more focus on the US housing sector, which is considered by many to be a solid indicator of the health of the US economy overall. The market is hungry for information on when the US economy is likely to turn around, and the construction of new housing (quoted in 'housing units' by the US Census Bureau) is seen as a good indicator of the health of the underlying US economy. In other countries different figures are used to assess the health of the housing sector. For example, in the UK it is mortgage approvals or one of the key benchmarks on house prices, like that published by Nationwide.

Budget

We looked earlier in this chapter at how national debt and government borrowing can affect a currency. A budget – a government's spending and taxation plan – can also be closely studied by FX markets. This will indicate how close a government is likely to be to balancing its budget. Generally speaking, the market likes to see governments spending within their limits: a massive borrowing programme, particularly an unanticipated one, can see traders selling a currency fast.

Manufacturing/industrial production figures

Various measures are regularly published covering the rate at which a country's factories are producing new goods. Busy factories mean not only that there is demand from the underlying economy, but also that exports may be on the up. This will be good news for the currency over the medium to long term. Different indicators will govern manufacturing in different countries: the ISM Manufacturing Index in the US is closely followed by many FX traders, while the OECD *Main Economic Indicators* report covers many of the other major markets. The Producer Price Index (PPI) quoted for many economies

Sucden Financial

December 2011 Calendar

Last updated 30/11/2011

KEY
FN: First Notice Day
LT: Last Trading Day
OE: Option Expiry
DE: Germany
EZ: Europe
JP: Japan
CN: China

Monday	Tuesday	Wednesday	Thursday	Friday
5 0855 DE Nov Services PMI 0900 EZ Nov Services PMI 0930 UK Nov Services PMI 1000 EZ Oct Retail Sales 1500 US Oct Factory Orders 1500 US Nov ISM Non-Manufacturing OE: Dec Gasoil (ICE)	**6** 0001 UK Nov BRC Retail Sales 1000 EZ Q3 GDP 1100 DE Oct Industrial Orders 1500 US Dec IBD Sentiment	**7** 0500 JP Oct Leading Index 0930 UK Oct Ind. & Man. Production 1100 DE Oct Industrial Production 1500 US NIESR GDP Estimate 1530 US w/e EIA Energy Stocks 2000 US Oct Consumer Credit	**1** 0100 CN Nov Manufacturing PMI 0230 CN Nov HSBC Manufacturing PMI 0855 DE Nov Manufacturing PMI 0900 EZ Nov Manufacturing PMI 0930 UK Nov Manufacturing PMI 1330 US Nov Jobless Claims 1500 US Nov ISM Manufacturing 1500 US Oct Construction Spending 1530 US w/e EIA Nat Gas OE:	**2** 1000 EZ Oct PPI 1330 US Nov NF Payrolls & Unemployment OE: Jan Cocoa (NYBOT) FN: Dec Heating Oil (NYMEX)
12 10/12 CN Nov Imports, Exports & Trade Bal 0300 CN Oct New Yuan Loans & Money Supply 1900 US Nov Fed Budget LT: Dec Gasoil (ICE) OE: Jan Brent Crude (ICE)	**13** 0930 UK Nov RICS House Prices 0930 UK Oct DCLG House Prices 0930 UK Nov CPI & RPI 1000 DE Dec ZEW Index 1330 US Nov Retail Sales 1500 US Oct Business Inventories 1915 US Dec Fed Rate LT: Dec Cocoa (LIFFE)	**14** 0430 JP Oct Ind. Production 0930 UK Nov Claimant Count 0930 UK Oct Av. Earnings & ILO Unempt 1000 EZ Oct Ind Production 1330 US Nov CPI 1530 US w/e EIA Energy Stocks 2350 JP Q4 Tankan LT: Dec Soy Complex, Corn, Wheat (CBOT) FN: Dec Cocoa (NYBOT)	**8** 1200 UK Dec BoE Rate 1245 EZ Dec ECB Rate 1330 US Nov Jobless Claims 1500 US Oct Wholesale Inventories 1530 US w/e EIA Nat Gas	**9** 0200 CN Nov CPI & PPI 0200 CN Nov Industrial Production 0200 CN Nov Retail Sales 0700 DE Nov Trade Bal 0700 DE Oct Imports & Exports 0700 DE Nov CPI 0930 UK Oct Trade Bal & Non EU 0930 UK Nov PPI Core 0930 UK Nov Input and Output 1330 US Oct Trade Bal 1330 US Dec Michigan Survey 1455 US OE: Jan Coffee (NYBOT)
19 0001 UK Dec Rightmove House Prices 0900 EZ Oct Invest Flow & c/a LT: Dec Coffee (NYBOT)	**20** 0001 UK Dec GfK survey 0001 DE Dec IFO - Current Assessment 0900 DE Dec IFO - Business Climate 1330 US Nov Housing starts LT: Jan Crude - WTI (NYMEX)	**21** 0001 UK Dec Bbu Rate 0700 DE Nov PSNCR & PSNB 0930 UK Nov PSNCR & PSNB 0930 UK Dec BOE minutes 1500 US Nov Existing Homes Sales 1530 US w/e EIA Energy Stocks OE: Jan Coffee (LIFFE)	**15** 0930 UK Nov Retail sales 1330 US Nov PPI 1330 US Nov NY Fed Manufacturing 1330 US Nov Jobless Claims 1415 US Nov Ind Prod & Capacity Use 1500 US Nov Michigan Survey 1530 US w/e EIA Nat Gas LT: Dec Crude WTI (NYMEX) OE: Jan Sugar (NYBOT)	**16** 1000 EZ Oct Trade Balance 1330 US Nov CPI & Real Earnings LT: Dec FTSE 100 Index OE: Dec FTSE 100 Index & Equity (LIFFE)
26 US & UK Market Holiday 0001 UK Dec Homeback Housing Survey	**27** UK Market Holiday 1500 US Dec Rich Fed 1500 US Dec Consumer Confidence 1330 US Dec Midwest Manufacturing 2330 JP Nov CPI 2350 JP Nov Retail Sales OE: Dec Copper (COMEX) Jan Heating oil, Rbob & Nat Gas (NYMEX)	**28** 1530 US w/e EIA Energy Stocks LT: Dec Copper, Gold, Silver (COMEX) Jan Natural Gas (NYMEX)	**22** 0930 US Q3 GDP 1330 US Nov Chicago Fed 1330 US Nov Personal consumption 1330 US Q3 GDP & PCE 1330 US Nov Jobless Claims 1465 US Nov Michigan Survey 1500 US Nov Lead Indicators 1530 US w/e EIA Nat Gas FN: Jan Crude - WTI (NYMEX)	**23** JP Market Holiday 1330 US Nov PCE & Personal income 1330 US Nov Durable Gds & New Orders 1500 US Nov New Homes OE: Jan Soy Complex, Corn, Wheat (CBOT)
			29 0900 EZ Nov M3 & Private loans 1330 US Nov Jobless Claims 1445 US Dec Chicago PMI 1500 US Nov Pending Home Sales 1530 US w/e EIA Nat Gas 1600 US Dec KC Fed LT: Jan Natural Gas (NYMEX) FN: Jan Natural Gas (NYMEX)	**30** 1500 US Dec NAPM-NY LT: Jan Heating oil, RBOB (NYMEX) FN: Jan Copper, Gold, Silver (COMEX) OE: Jan Soy Complex (CBOT) Jan Cocoa (LIFFE)

Table 6.1 Sucden Financial economic calendar December 2011 (www.sucdenfinancial.com)

will show what sort of price producers are getting for the goods that they manufacture. It can be a good early warning sign of a slowing or contracting economy. The OECD publishes a PPI for most of the developed world economies and many of the emerging ones, too.

A typical economic calendar (December 2011)

Table 6.1 is a good example of a typical economic calendar published by Sucden Financial (www.sucdenfinancial.com). It shows how much is going on in terms of published data in the course of the month of December. Two-letter prefixes show you which country is publishing the data. DE is Germany, CN is China. The calendar also helpfully tells the trader at what point during the day the information is being published.

Even if you are more of a technical trader and spend less time analysing underlying economic data, it is still worth knowing whether any major announcements are coming up, as they represent potential bumps in the road if the data are unexpected in nature.

Utilitarian considerations

At this point it is still worth emphasising that many participants in the FX market are *not* traders, or central banks for that matter. They are ordinary businesses buying and selling currency in order to meet their day-to-day foreign currency needs. They are not speculating on price. Take the example of the Japanese insurance companies buying yen in order to meet domestic claims after the March 2011 earthquake. They *had* to buy yen and they *had* to buy it in March. Their activity, en masse, was enough to move the yen up against the US dollar.

Not all of the above indicators are considered as being equally important all of the time. Traders will focus on some indicators when they are anticipating the economic situation will deteriorate, and will look at others when they are expecting signs of growth.

7

Developing a trading plan for currency markets

Are profitable currency traders born or made? It is a question that continues to engage investing circles. In 1983, a famous Chicago-based money manager called Richard Dennis bet his colleague William Eckhardt that it was possible to train novice traders from scratch. He recruited 23 people off the street, with no trading experience, and taught them how to become profitable traders. This was the beginning of his so-called 'Turtle' programme.

Not all of the Turtles succeeded, but enough did for Dennis to entrust them with millions of his own money and for them to go on to generate more than $175 million in profits in the next five years. A few went on to become successful money managers in their own right. You can read more about Dennis and this experiment in Curtis M. Faith's *Way of the Turtle* (2007).

Dennis and Eckhardt both had a point. Dennis was not training his Turtles to find their own way to invest, he was teaching them to trade a system of his own devising. It was essential, he argued, to follow the system, to be disciplined, to avoid distractions, in order to profit.

More recently, BBC television broadcast *Million Dollar Traders* followed a similar experiment as a fly-on-the-wall documentary, with eight ordinary individuals being taught to become traders and in the end trading real money.

What both experiments illustrated was that while trading can be taught, not everyone is mentally suited to trading. People might think they are, but your emotional and psychological building blocks really determine your ability to trade successfully.

Having said that, there are many different approaches to trading financial markets, and it is possible that you may favour one approach over another. In this chapter we ask a few questions of you, the novice currency trader, which may help you to find the trading approach that will suit you, your financial resources and your lifestyle.

How much can I afford to lose?

This is probably one of the most important questions you will need to ask yourself before you begin live trading. Before opening a trading account, it is crucial that you have a very clear idea of how much money you can afford to lose. What is the maximum loss you can sustain before you walk away? You will always need to have this in mind because the last thing you want to do is to trade with money that you need for other things.

Money management is part of the discipline of being a good trader. Remember, if your initial pool of trading capital starts diminishing, perhaps after a few early losses, you will need to alter your position sizes to compensate. If you start trading currency markets with $5,000, and you lose $1,000, then your position sizes will need to be 20 per cent smaller to compensate. Otherwise, you are ramping up your risk and could suffer larger proportional losses later on. Your risk management must always inform your trading process, certainly in terms of the size of the bets you take on.

While working in the CFD trading industry, it was repeatedly made clear to me that many people viewed CFD trading as a way to make a quick buck. They would risk rainy-day money, such as a $20,000 college fund, for example, in the hopes of making an additional few thousand dollars. They ended up losing cash which they needed for other things. Don't let this happen to you. Only trade FX with money you can afford to lose.

How much time can I devote to trading?

The amount of time you can afford to devote to trading forex will dictate your trading style. Many successful professional traders claim they spend 90 per cent of their time doing research, educating themselves about the markets, rather than simply sitting in front of a screen watching prices. You will see traders at big banks glued to their screens, but that is because they are being paid to sit there by their employer. It is a popular misconception that the more time you spend sitting in front of a computer, the more likely you are to make money.

I once visited a trading company in Gibraltar which rented desk space and infrastructure to self-employed derivatives traders. It was interesting to see that some clients were spending all day in front of their screens, executing hundreds of individual trades, while others would come in first thing in the morning, catch up on overnight news, place a few trades (with stops in place, of course) and then go to the beach.

One of the reasons so many housewives are now successful traders is because they have the time and flexibility to match a trading program to their lifestyle commitments. They are often up early, so can put trades on before the school run, and can monitor their positions during the day.

Currency markets are well suited to the modern lifestyle because they are open around the clock and you can check up on them in the evening instead of watching television. You are not limited by the opening and closing time of stock exchanges. The markets are almost always live, letting you trade when it suits you.

Your approach to currency trading will be dictated by the time you can usefully apply to it. Mobile technology now makes it easier to keep tabs on your positions while you are on the move and can alert you to sudden changes, so there's no need to be anchored to your desk. But many people are able to sustain a successful strategy with only 30 minutes or so of focus time per day.

How do I behave under pressure?

'Know thyself', said the ancient Greek inscription at the Temple of Delphi, and this aphorism is particularly valid for trading. Don't kid yourself. Know your weaknesses. The markets will not – ever – cut you any slack. So it is crucial that you are honest with yourself when trading. In particular, how do you behave under pressure? Are you a risk taker, or would you describe yourself as cautious?

Some traders are over-confident. They can set off into trading in the belief that they are right, the markets are wrong, and within months they'll be placing a down payment on a new Porsche. That rarely – if ever – happens. Some of the cleverest, most numerate people on the planet have been caught out by financial markets. If you feel you might be a tad over-pleased with yourself in your day-to-day life, be honest with yourself and apply that to the way you trade. Ask yourself constantly whether this aspect of your personality is creeping into the way you trade.

Similarly, if you are a naturally cautious person, be aware of how this can affect your trading. Are you placing your stops too close to the market? Are you hesitating to put a trade on and then kicking yourself when it comes good and you weren't in the market? Are you getting out of your trades too early and losing out on potential profits?

Those who may have a tendency to gamble anyway need to think very carefully about approaching currency trading. It may be considered in some quarters as gambling, but unlike gambling it brings with it additional risk factors in terms of the margin aspect. If you are the sort of person who nips in and out of betting shops on a regular basis, you may be best advised to stay away from currency trading.

How disciplined am I as an individual?

Trading requires discipline. If you are not a disciplined person, then you need to get strict with yourself when it comes to trading, because at the end of the day it will be you who will carry the costs of poor market discipline. Once you have a trading plan in place, stick to it. Don't try to find ways around it, or argue yourself out of it. Once you begin doing this, it is a slippery slope towards disaster.

A very experienced trader once sat me down and tried to convince me that his losing position in the shares of an oil company was going to come good. He made a complex case using technical analysis, but it was not convincing – most ways you looked at his position, it seemed as if it was going to lose more money. He was refusing to cut his losses, clinging to a share that would, in the end, cost him more money. He was looking to me to provide independent confirmation of his technical thesis. He had already half-convinced himself he was right, but the reason he was doing this was the loss he had already sustained: he could not bear to 'wear' it and instead was clinging to a losing position.

If you have a trading programme, and you stick to it, you are less likely to find yourself trying to convince yourself in the wee hours of the morning that a losing position will come good. If you feel you are an undisciplined, lax or chaotic person, make sure you write a trading programme and stick to it religiously. There's nothing wrong with tweaking it later on, but again, be disciplined about when you tweak it. Don't change it just because that would suit where you are in the market right now. It is like being on a diet: no dairy products means *no dairy products* not no dairy products but maybe cheese on Sundays.

Let's say you decide to limit losses to a certain percentage of the total value of the trade, 5 per cent for example. You write in your plan that after exactly two months you will revisit it. After two months you notice that the market you are trading has rallied a fair few times just after you came out. You review your overall risk position and decide you can tolerate a 7 per cent loss threshold. But you are doing this at the point when you decided to review the plan, not when you have a 5 per cent loss on a trade and want to give yourself the opportunity to let it run.

Writing a trading plan

Some trading plans can be extremely sophisticated. As someone starting out, with perhaps a couple of FX demo accounts, you don't need an incredibly complex approach, but you do need something written down. Don't just blunder into trading FX markets, because you will be taken apart in fairly short order.

A trading plan, like a business plan, also helps you to focus on some core issues of your approach to currency markets. It makes you think about what it is you are setting out to do before you get close to opening your first forex trade. It can also be useful as an exercise later in your trading career, if you have sustained some consistent losses, helping you to take a step away from the market to revisit your approach.

What follows are just some of the main questions you need to answer in your trading plan. Every trader is different and so is every trading plan. But some of the key issues ought to be addressed in each trading plan.

What is it I want to trade?

Which currency pairs are you going to concentrate on? Most beginners will start off focusing on one of the majors, like EUR/USD or USD/JPY, and graduate onto other pairs when they feel more confident and when they see some kind of price action. In addition, you will need to decide what sort of format you will use for your currency trading – this will largely depend on where you live and the degree to which you feel comfortable trading forex on margin. Most seasoned FX traders seem to recommend trading multiple currency pairs rather than focusing slavishly on just one or two markets. They are often hunting for momentum characteristics across 10 or more FX pairs and will then zero in on a market where they see something interesting happening.

How much money am I going to risk?

Only risk money you can afford to lose. Determine how much trading capital you are going to allocate to FX trading and finance your account with that. But remember: don't risk more than 5 per cent of this on trades, if that. The size of your trading account will also determine the maximum size of trade risk you take on. Even £500 out of £5,000 trading capital is probably risking too much.

When am I going to trade?

Take a long, hard look at your lifestyle and decide how much time you think you can put towards trading. This will influence your strategy heavily. You may want to devote an hour every day, or plan to trade on the move, for example when commuting on the train. You may have the luxury of being able to trade all day long. There is no hard and fast answer to how much time should be devoted on a daily basis to trading currency markets: you can be just as effective on 30 minutes a day as spending all day in front of your trading screen, if not more so.

How long am I prepared to keep each trade open?

The pure day-trading strategy will see the trader closing out all his positions, even the losing ones, every day. This is a good discipline in a way, as it stops the trader from hanging onto a lost position and increasing that loss over time. It also limits the ability to win big on some other trades. A good trading plan should therefore inform the reader of what you intend to do with both winning and losing positions. If there is a time limit to these, particularly losing ones, it can help you to manage the downside risk.

How many trades will I keep open at a time?

Don't let brokers encourage you to have too many positions open at a time. A currency hedge fund can run 3,000 trades a day on its computers, but that's a billion-dollar operation. The private trader will never have close to these resources. Have only as many positions as you feel you can monitor effectively. Beginners should have only one or two active positions open at a time. After that, much will depend on what you're comfortable with and whether you have a strategy which depends on high-frequency trading or whether you prefer more of a momentum approach.

Will I keep trades open when I am away from my trading screen?

This is a big consideration, as some strategies may require the trader to keep a close eye on the markets. You can automate some of the process using automated orders with your brokerage, but that can take you only so far. Walking away from live positions in the market can be hard to do early on, but if you are managing your risk properly, you should not be losing any sleep. Like with cooking, some strategies need more hands-on management than others.

What will I do with the money I make?

Will you keep your winnings inside your trading account or will you bank them? There is an argument for continuing to build your trading account over time, allowing you to open larger trades and in the end make more money. But a string of losses can also upset that. One approach is to set a maximum size for your trading account, a target you work towards that will allow you to open trades of a size you are personally comfortable with, and then bank any profits above that.

How will I assess my trading performance?

What sort of benchmarks will you put in place to help you analyse your trading performance? Keeping a trade journal is considered good practice among many traders. It helps you to look back on the trades you have made in the past, why you made them, and what the results were. It also allows you to assess on a weekly or monthly basis what your profit and loss looked like. This is considered critical if you want to learn from your mistakes, and to assess your performance as a trader. It is also helpful intelligence should you ever consider retaining a trading coach to help you to tackle recurring problems in your approach to currency markets.

Is FX trading going to be my career, my hobby, or a way of making money on the side?

Have a clear idea of what it is you want to get out of trading. For me, it has always been an intellectual interest in financial markets, which is what got me into financial journalism in the first place. For others, it is a way to make some extra money, get out of the rat race, or fill long bouts of insomnia.

Your trading strategy should be one that has a good chance of meeting your expectations. If you are going to make only a few hundred dollars extra per month, it is unlikely to be a way for you to ditch the day job. Be realistic about what it can achieve for you financially. With the best will in the world, you won't be able to turn a $10,000 trading account into $200,000 overnight. You will need to work hard at it, and it may take months or years. FX trading is not like winning the lottery: it won't make you rich overnight.

Some people with large quantities of available cash are able to make big profits as well, but they start off with a six-figure account. Working up to there from a smaller starting point will take time and a considerable dose of luck. On the upside, as a hobby, trading can be a lot more profitable than owning a yacht!

Am I a trader or an investor?

An investor is someone who buys something in the expectation that it will go up in value over time, may even pay them a stream of income, and can be sold for a profit at some yet to be determined point in the future. Investors like to accrue assets over time. They are canny money managers, often with a good eye for a bargain. They like investing in shares, because shares pay dividends and give them a stake in a viable corporate entity. They like houses, because they are made of bricks and mortar, and can be rented out to tenants.

Traders are focused on much shorter timescales. They think in minutes, days or weeks. They are looking for price action, the possibility for sudden and large changes in the value of assets. Traders like futures markets and FX trading because they don't need to shoulder the costs of owning an asset: there are no custody fees associated with a currency pair. Traders generally have a higher risk tolerance than investors.

Many investors venture into FX trading because it is often advertised or promoted alongside traditional investment services such as share dealing. But some investors find themselves unsuited to currency markets. And just because you have made a lot of money as an investor does not mean you will be successful as a trader. There are some investors who also make good traders, but not everyone can be a Warren Buffett and a George Soros at the same time.

In addition, I would advise that if you are a successful investor, don't risk too much of your investment capital on FX markets. At times it will seem that forex is one of the few ways to make money in an uncertain market. The nature of currency markets is such that there is always a winning and a losing currency in any trade, so there is, by definition, always scope for making money. But at the same time, most FX accounts don't provide you with the scope for owning an asset. If your objective is long-term capital gain, perhaps coupled with a degree of income, I would suggest looking elsewhere.

Approaching the markets

Day trading

In the 1990s the day-trading phenomenon sprang up in the US. Between 1992 and 2000, global equity markets were in a very long and very profitable bull trend. It was easy for people with a solid chunk of starting capital to make money and earn a living by trading share markets. They were known as day traders because they spent all day trading.

Today it is not quite as easy to make money in the markets. They are more volatile, and subject to pressures that did not exist in the 1990s.

Prices are affected by market participants – such as hedge funds, for example – that were much smaller and less influential 15 years ago. Day traders still exist, and many still trade for a living, but the day-trading strategy referred to here is where a trader will close out his positions by the time the market closes. There are no positions held overnight.

As a lifestyle call, day trading can be attractive because it means you can spend some days trading and some days on the golf course or doing something else more fascinating. You aren't worrying about what your trading account is doing while you're teeing off at the seventh. It also means that during those days when you are trading, you can be focused on the market.

From a psychological perspective, day trading is also useful if you're not feeling like trading when you wake up. You can leave the market alone and come back to it another day. It is also easy for day traders to determine how they're doing performance-wise: either they're up or they're down when they close out. The key is making sure there are more up days than down days.

Day-trading strategies are necessarily very short term in nature. Some involve putting on a number of positions at the start of the day, while others deal with entering and exiting the market at the right moments in the course of the day (so-called intra-day moves). High-frequency trading can be expensive, however, as spreads can be so wide you will end up coughing up a big chunk of your gains. Luckily, spreads on currencies are relatively tight when compared with other, less liquid markets, such as shares. Be careful if developing a day-trading strategy that involves dozens of trades per day unless the spread is amazingly narrow. You may find you end up with little real gain to show for it, although your currency broker will be pleased.

Trend following

Trend following is one of the most popular trading strategies and can work if you are a short-term or long-term trader, although most successful trend followers tend to lean towards the longer end of the time frame. In a nutshell, trend followers use technical analysis to seek out trends in markets and gradually build their exposure over time. If the trend looks like it has 'legs' to it and will run, they increase the position. If it begins to look as though it is running out of steam, they start to reduce their exposure. Trend followers tend to rely on moving averages as one of the key indicators of an emerging trend.

Patience is critical for the successful trend follower. They like to be fairly certain that a trend has emerged before they open a trade. This means giving up some early gains in return for the ability to ride the trend up (or down if it is a short trend). Once they become more pessimistic about the trend, they might close their original position and then open a smaller, more conservative position. This way they have managed to lock in some of the original value of the trade and reduce their overall exposure in case the trend reverses.

Trend followers will shop around across a number of markets in search of the right trend. However, there will be times in the markets when good trends are simply absent and it will become very difficult to make money consistently this way. Some seasoned traders will take this opportunity to simply go on holiday and come back when things have settled down. Trying to trade as a trend follower during periods of high volatility and market uncertainty is never a good idea.

Some of the great trends in recent history in the FX markets have included the following:

- The big fall in the value of the US dollar against the Japanese yen has been a long-term trend favoured by many FX traders. Starting at around 95 to the dollar, the yen has been trying to strengthen at every opportunity since then. There was a major downwards trend in the USD/JPY pair in Q2 and Q3 of 2010. Since then the pair has become more range bound (bouncing between two price levels) as the Bank of Japan, the central bank, has sought to keep the currency cheaper by intervening in the market (selling yen and buying dollars).

■ The fall in the EUR in the early stages of the European sovereign debt crisis. The EUR weakened from about 1.245 dollars at the beginning of March 2009 as concerns began to grow about the debt status of some Eurozone countries to hit a nadir at 1.514 before it began to strengthen again. This was a good trend for FX traders – there was a soft trend downwards for the EUR against the USD from July through to mid-October 2009, before the EUR began to gradually strengthen again as the focus switched to the struggling US economy. This time traders were able to go long EUR against the dollar, as it gained ground to peak at around 1.96 dollars in June 2010.

■ The dramatic fall in the value of the pound in the final quarter of 2008 turned into a big earner for some foreign exchange traders. Sterling fell against the euro, for example, from about 1.29 to almost parity at 1.02. The market for sterling then became much more choppy and unpredictable in 2009, and the trend evaporated almost before all the mince pies from Christmas had been eaten.

■ The rise of the Swissie against the USD during 2011. In this case the CHF strengthened from 1.175 in June 2010, reaching 0.71 in August 2011 at the height of the US federal funding crisis and the US debt downgrade. Its course was then dramatically reversed by the intervention of the Swiss central bank.

Swing trading

In Chapter 8 we look briefly at how some markets can become range bound, i.e. the price never seems to break above a certain level, and seems to trade between two bands. This is the province of the swing trader, someone who uses the scope that FX trading offers to short markets as well as to go long.

Swing trading in its most basic form involves going long the market until it approaches a resistance level, then getting out, and eventually going short in expectation that it will turn slightly before or slightly after the resistance level. No market remains range bound for ever, so it is important that a stop loss is always in place to protect you when the price finally streaks out of the range.

Advanced swing traders use technical analysis and sometimes computer programs to help inform them about opportunities in the market. It is much more of a short-term strategy and many swing traders will be in and out of a trade in a matter of days. Unlike trend following, swing trading is more adaptable to volatile market periods.

Trading the news versus trading the technicals

Some FX traders like to trade the news. This means they are either reacting to announcements that have the potential to move a currency, or have a pretty good idea what a scheduled economic announcement will be and hence can take a position in advance. This can be very tricky and it is easy to lose money this way. This book includes an entire chapter on what it is exactly that moves currency markets, but suffice to say, when analysts and traders speak about 'trading the news' they are referring to a strategy which especially involves reacting to fundamental news in some form, whether in advance of it or once it is out.

Be aware that FX markets can 'gap' quite violently on the back of unexpected news – for example when a central bank governor holds a press conference and talks down the economy at a time when most analysts have been feeling quite positive. This can be enough to move a currency downwards quite rapidly.

Most trading coaches teaching a 'system' will prefer their pupils to ignore the news entirely, or at least use it only to flavour a more technical approach to forex markets. A technical trading strategy uses technical analysis to assess when to enter and exit the market and to evaluate when a trend is developing at a relatively early stage.

There is a broad range of technical overlays you can apply to a particular currency market. We go into more detail on some of the more frequently used models later in this book. Nobody makes use of everything, but some overlays, such as moving averages and pattern recognition, seem to have gained considerable traction with the bulk of the FX trading community.

A pure technical approach to FX trading is divorced entirely from the news. The analyst or trader is looking at his FX charts without even glancing at the Reuters news feed. It is really a case of isolating patterns and trends and exploiting them.

Intermarket trading

This approach to the markets, pioneered by the likes of John Murphy and Lou Mendelsohn, uses the study of one or more markets to inform trading decisions in another. The analyst seeks signals from other markets to inform currency trading decisions. For example, looking at the yield curve on government debt securities or the price of gold might provide some insight into the performance of the USD. This is a highly technical approach to markets and requires a fairly broad knowledge of the financial markets beyond currency markets, as well as how central banks manage money supply.

Another good example is the CAD (Canadian dollar) and the price of crude oil. The Canadian dollar is one of the so-called resource currencies: because Canada is a major exporter of natural resources, such as oil, grain, base metals and so forth, its currency often performs in line with major commodity markets. If the CAD was seen to diverge significantly from the oil price, for example, an intermarket strategist might look for some kind of reversion towards the oil price. A rising CAD when oil prices are falling might reveal a short-term opportunity.

A successful intermarket strategy requires a degree of consistency. In the above example, you would need to see a pattern emerging over a period of time, with previous examples of the currency behaving in the way you expect it to perform.

Systematic trading

Many traders now deploy systematic approaches to currency trading, thanks again in part to the round-the-clock nature of the market, and the fact that the prices of the major currency pairs are seen as fairly efficient expressions of value. These usually require some form of computer program, some of which are commercially available, although some simpler systems can be executed manually.

Trading systems are useful in that they enforce discipline: the human trader is almost taking a step back from the market and focusing purely on making sure the system is properly managed. It means there is less emotion involved, as computer programs don't get ruffled by having the market turn against them suddenly.

A typical system will inform the trader when to buy and when to sell, based on signals from the market. It is important to recognise that no system is infallible, however. Markets change, and a program written 10 years ago to trade GBP/USD is not necessarily going to work as well trading EUR/JPY today. Some professional currency traders actually use two or more systems, for example a low-volatility program which switches to a high-volatility methodology when the markets change speed.

Some FX brokerages offer trading programs – also called expert advisers – as part of their service. These often come with an additional fee, or are reserved for clients prepared to deposit US$10,000 or more. Some pretty outlandish claims are made for some of these. For example, one recent engine was claimed to have been able to turn US$2,000 into more than a million in less than three months. But ask yourself this: if it were that easy to give a computer US$2,000 and receive over a million three months later, why isn't every hedge fund on the planet doing the same thing? If this program was ever able to achieve this feat, it was likely a one-off event, possibly benefiting from a sudden gap in the market. Being positioned in the right place at the right time can certainly help in this respect.

I would take most of the claims made by purveyors of expert advisers with a large pinch of salt. They may have their uses – for example, managing part of your account overnight – but I'd be loath to simply plug a computer into a $10,000 margined forex account and walk away from it.

Hedge funds that use a highly systematic approach to FX markets spend a lot of time and money fine tuning their systems. One programmer told me that it is never possible to achieve perfection in this respect because ultimately the market will change and the computer program will not be able to adapt. This is why there is a never-ending stream of FX trading engines coming out: the program that made a lot of money trading Cable in 2010 will not necessarily be so adept at it in 2012.

8

Technical analysis for the FX trader

Once you start researching forex markets you will quickly come across people using what will seem like a bewildering array of charts and graphs to analyse markets. This process is known as 'technical analysis', and the people who rely on charts for their investment decisions are sometimes called 'chartists'.

Technical analysis has been around from some time now, but it is gathering more adherents every month. The more traders who use technical analysis to buy and sell, the more accurate it becomes, as everyone uses the same factors. It is almost a self-fulfilling method of following markets.

On its own, technical analysis is not going to turn you into a millionaire overnight. It is really a tool to help you to determine when to enter and exit markets, and when a trend you are following is likely to reverse. In this chapter we will look at some of the more widely used charts. It is the tip of the iceberg really. There are hundreds of different theories out there about how to analyse markets. If it is something you would like to learn more about, further ideas for reading are provided in this book's bibliography.

'Technical analysis is not about forecasting', according to Michael van Dulken, a research analyst at Accendo Markets. 'It is all based on the price ... you want to make a bet on the market, but you want that bet to be the best it can be. You're looking for things that support your view, and the more you can find, the better.'

The background to technical analysis

Technical analysis in western financial markets was really born with the observations of the US stock market made by Charles Dow in the early 1900s. Dow was part-owner and editor of *The Wall Street Journal*. He observed that the US share market tended often to move before news that affected it became available. Looking at the market in aggregate, it was unthinkable that the entire market could be manipulated in this fashion. Ergo, it was potentially possible to predict price movements in advance of news, or indeed in advance of the major moves. This in turn began to reinforce the case for studying price movements in a more technical fashion, on the strength that, beyond individual stocks, and over longer periods of time, the price should reflect all the market news.

There is not the space here to explore efficient markets theory – other publications have already done a good job of that – but the crux of what Dow and his successors were after was a means to catch trends and reversals early, before the rest of the market piled in. Too often we hear stories about how retail traders are always the last to buy into a bull market, just as it peaks, leaving them more often than not saddled with a loss. We hear about the canny hedge fund managers who are first into a market and make millions thanks to their prescience. But much of this boils down to being an astute observer of the markets, and using the right tools to assess them.

At its most basic, technical analysis involves looking at resistance and support indicators. A typical currency pair will often move between two price levels – an upper (resistance) and lower (support) limit. It will seem as if whenever it reaches the support level, it will take off again and will top out as it gets to the upper limit. Why is this, you may wonder? Is there a big seller out there automatically off-loading stock whenever the price hits a certain level?

The reality is that many market participants, including professional and amateur traders, funds, banks, market makers, you name it, are all looking at the same prices: resistance levels (a particular price point at which the market is likely to turn from an upward trend back to a downward one) and support levels (the exact opposite – the price below which the market could reverse direction as more buyers come in).

Resistance and support levels also act as 'floors' in a market – they are a means of forecasting when there is a likely change of direction, even though this may not change an overall trend. If a trader is focusing on short, intra-day price movements, they can still be important indicators.

Figure 8.1   Currency pair showing law of 50s and 100s

The reason these levels exist is because they represent the price beyond which the market will buy or sell as it perceives the price becoming too high or too low. It is not just one big trader causing this (although there are some examples in the history of financial markets when it has been), it is hundreds or thousands of traders all reacting the same way. In forex markets in particular, the sheer volume of trading that goes on makes it harder for a single participant to move the market consistently.

In the end, a currency pair can become range bound – effectively bouncing between two price levels. If it breaks beyond one of these – a 'breakout' – it can cause excitement, as traders and analysts come to the conclusion that the price is moving on towards a new resistance level.

Resistance levels are important when trading; one is tempted to scoff at them initially, but they are very real and need to be watched closely. Without other fundamental news to drive prices, resistance levels can begin to dominate things, as traders focus on particular price levels. They can often be nice round numbers because that is how humans think.

A good example in FX markets is the law of 50s and 100s (see Figure 8.1) – currency pairs often develop artificial resistance levels where the last two digits are '00' or '50'. Why is this? My theory is that a large slice of currency hedging and currency management is being carried on in a semi-automated manner by some very large market participants that are simply too lazy to use irregular price points for their buy and sell orders.

Japanese candlestick charts

Japanese candlestick charts have been used in East Asia since the 1600s, when they were first employed by rice traders. They have been adopted in the West only relatively recently, first being brought to the attention of analysts by Steve Nison in his 1991 book *Japanese Candlestick Charting Techniques*. These charts are not for everyone, but I've found that once you start looking at markets with candlesticks, you never go back.

A Japanese candlestick is a measure of what the market did over a certain period of time, be it a minute, an hour, or a day (see Figure 8.2). It really depends on which timescale you are viewing the market from. A single candlestick will show you four pieces of information: the highest point the price reached during that time period, the lowest point, and the open and closing prices.

The top and bottom of the fat part of the candlestick are the price the market opened and the price it closed. The narrow line goes as high as the highest price point reached, and vice versa, the line beneath traces the lowest price. Thus, if your market closing price was also the lowest price, you would not have a 'tail' to your candlestick. A very long candle is indicative of plenty of volatile moves, while a short, fat one is an indicator of a market which did not do much.

Source: Alpari

Figure 8.2 Sample Japanese candlestick graph created in the MetaTrader 4 platform

I say opening and closing price, as if talking about a single day in the market, and certainly you could look at a share market in this way, with each candlestick representing a single day. However, this is not relevant for FX markets, and many analysts use them for shorter timescales anyway, with the candlestick representing an hour or a 10-minute interval. When analysing forex markets in particular, where there is no market close per se, a candlestick is a useful measure of what has been happening on an hour-by-hour basis.

As you can see, candlesticks provide you with much more information than simply a line on a chart.

Moving averages

A moving average (MA) is a line calculated using the average of past prices, but updated every day (or hour, or minute, or second, depending on the time period you are using). Taking a 20-day moving average as an example, your program is creating a line where each price point is the average of the prices of the previous 20 days. Other popular time periods are the 50-day moving average and the 200-day moving average.

The moving average helps the trader to identify a trend. If a price moves below a 20-day moving average having stayed above it for a long time, it might be a sell signal. In combination, two moving averages – the 20-day and the 50-day, for example – can provide a higher conviction indicator that a trend has been broken and a market is about to suffer a reversal. If, say, the price crosses the 20-day MA *and* the 50-day MA, then the market may well be heading for a fall.

The above are also referred to as simple moving averages because there is also another type – the weighted moving average. This type of MA will place greater emphasis on more recent price activity. It seeks to skirt around the problem that MAs suffer from – they rely heavily on historical data and are not as quick to react to reversals. Impatient traders and analysts who want to be able to react faster to possible changes use the weighted moving average to give them the extra time to exploit a move in price before the rest of the market.

Finally, an exponential moving average will take into consideration all the prices in the data series, but the earlier data are given far less significance than the most recent prices.

Traders will use a combination of MAs to determine whether they are really seeing an emerging new trend or just a false dawn. If there is a crossover, with the price crossing multiple moving averages, this can be a buy or sell signal (depending on which way the market is moving).

While the simple moving average (SMA) is not a perfect predictor of future market behaviour, it ought to draw your attention to possible momentum opportunities, as illustrated in Figure 8.3. Note also that an actual crossover is not necessarily always needed: here the two SMAs moved close together before a big upwards move for the euro.

Last 03/09/2010 04:00.00 O=1.2817 H=1.2829 L = 1.2813 C = 1.2821

Source: www.forexyard.com

Figure 8.3   EUR/USD showing 5-day and 20-day simple moving averages and crossover

MACD (moving average convergence/ divergence)

The MACD is an oft-quoted measure of momentum. It takes a pair of moving averages and subtracts the short-term one from the longer-term one in an effort to create a momentum indicator. The analyst is trying to identify some signal of underlying momentum in a market.

It is meant to be able to identify both trend and momentum, hence its popularity.

Traders using the MACD will be looking for signals to get into or out of a market, including crossovers. For example, they might use the MACD with a moving average of the MACD (called the 'trigger' line). When the MACD falls below the trigger line, this can indicate it is time to sell. When it climbs above the trigger line, it could be time to buy.

The MACD tends to be favoured by analysts focusing on equity markets rather than other types of financial market. Having said that, some forex traders claim to have enjoyed success using the MACD as well.

Bollinger bands

Bollinger bands are most often used as a way to analyse what a market is doing in the short term, for example intra-day. Most technical indicators are more efficient when used to identify trends and rever-

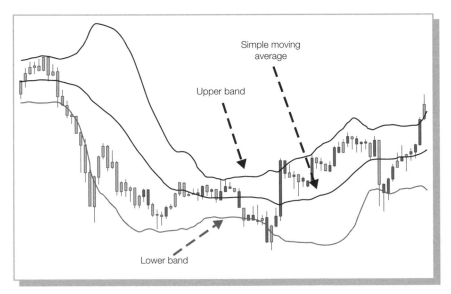

Source: www.forexindicator.org

Figure 8.4   Bollinger bands

sals over longer time periods. Bollinger bands are created using an exponential moving average (see moving averages, above) with two other lines above and below it based on the standard deviation of the market you are looking at.

If the market becomes more volatile, the bands will get wider apart. If it starts to trade tightly, they will get closer together again. The key is where the price of the market is compared with the bands. If it starts to get close to or even crosses the upper line, it may be time to start selling as the market is beginning to look overbought. If the price gets closer to the bottom line, it may be time to start buying. See Figure 8.4.

Head-and-shoulders indicators

You will probably hear chartists talking about the 'head and shoulders' of a market. This is one of the most popularly recognised patterns in financial markets, although there are many, many more, and we don't have the space to go into them in this book. However, head and shoulders does seem to have caught the imaginations of many technical analysts out there.

A head and shoulders pattern looks in its purest form like just that: two smaller peaks, with a higher peak in between. Analysts will see

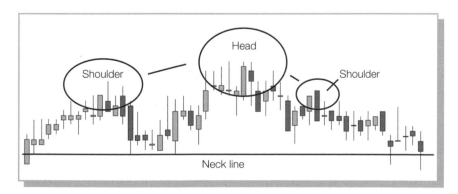

Figure 8.5   Head and shoulders pattern

one developing once a market has reached a peak and then dropped below the previous peak as well, and is then seen to be rising again. The assumption here is that the new peak will now be lower than the previous one. The market will not be able to achieve the same high again.

Analysts will be looking for the so-called neckline, a hypothetical line drawn between the dips on either side of the head (see Figure 8.5). After the right shoulder has formed, they expect the price will go down.

RSI (Relative Strength Index)

The Relative Strength Index is a popular measure used in conjunction with momentum – the speed at which a price is climbing or declining. Momentum is considered a better indicator of a bull market rather than a bear market, largely because markets tend to rise more than they fall – at least in the equities space. The RSI measures the speed at which prices are changing, again seeking that point where a market is overbought or oversold.

The RSI generates a figure of between zero and 100. If it is over 70, technical analysts begin to consider that currency as overbought or 'toppy' and start to look for signs that it will turn. If it is below 30, it is starting to look oversold and the price may be destined for an upturn. The RSI can sometimes be used in conjunction with other technical measures, such as momentum or moving averages, to look through the price action to find what is really going on with this particular share or market. It is used to try to filter out the 'noise' of a price jumping up and down, to discover what it is really doing.

ADX (Average Directional Index)

The Average Directional Index was designed by Welles Wilder, an American engineer, to analyse commodities markets, but as with many technical indicators, it can be used across a wide range of financial markets. It measures the momentum of a market, but what it does not tell you is whether the market is going up or down – all it is saying is that the market is moving.

The ADX is quoted in a range of 0–100 (see Figure 8.6). The higher it is, the more momentum you will be seeing. The lower, the more range bound that market now is. Generally speaking, if it is over 20, there is a trend in the market. If it drops below, the market is losing direction. You might see it cross the 20 or 30 mark as the market begins to take off, drop below it when it runs out of steam, and then pick up again as the market is sold off.

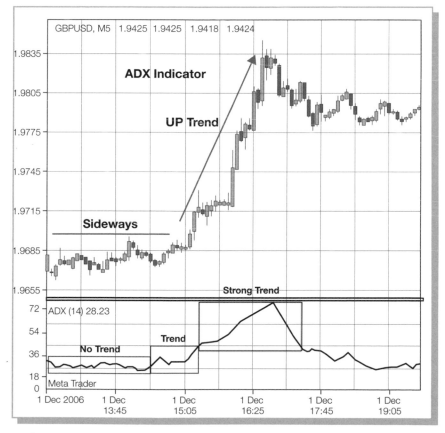

Source: www.aboutcurrency.com

Figure 8.6   **ADX versus GBP/USD**

The ADX is meant to help traders identify a trend in its early stages, before it becomes readily obvious on a normal chart. It is meant to tip them off to an opportunity to enter a market, or indeed to get out of one once it has lost its momentum.

Pivot points

Pivot points are often used in technical analysis to calculate support and resistance levels. A pivot point would typically be calculated using the averages of significant high points and low points of a previous trading period. There are a number of methods used by charting programs to work out pivot points, and much will depend on which time periods you are using to create them.

So how do we make use of pivot points? One method is as an indicator of trend-breaking momentum. If the market breaks out of the range established by the pivot points, this is a good indicator that some level of momentum has been achieved. Another approach is to use the pivot points to inform entry to and exit from the market. The trader can see at what price the market could be overbought or oversold. He/she can also set stop losses and limit orders using the price levels indicated by pivot points.

Two key points to bear in mind when using these are: firstly, this is a very short term indicator, and most traders will generally only use price information going back the last 24 hours. Pivot points seem to be less effective for weekly or monthly analysis timeframes, although some swing traders make use of them to establish their weekly trading ranges. Secondly, they, like other technical indicators, should not be viewed in isolation. Check them against other technical indicators like the MACD for example.

Let's say you're trading GBP/USD. You might then decide to use the daily behaviour of the currency pair as your time frame. Each day would therefore have its own pivot point based on what the pair did the day before. You could calculate it overnight or simply generate it at a touch of a button using a charting program.

Using the pivot points, technical analysts can also then begin to try to forecast resistance and support levels. Again, these levels will often be calculated using mathematical theories about markets, some of which are explained in more detail below. There is no completely accepted, carved-in-stone method of calculating pivot points, although there are a number that are in common use.

A common approach is to calculate a couple of resistance levels above the pivot point (e.g. one at 50 per cent and another at around 62 per cent above the pivot point) and a couple of support levels. This would then inform where you expect the market's turning points to be during that trading day.

Triangles

Triangles are often used when seeking a 'break-out' either to the upside or to the downside. They are drawn using a chart when the market looks like it is trading in an ever narrower range, i.e. forming a triangle. It can be illustrated by drawing two lines, ideally with price peaks and troughs touching the long sides of the triangle 2–5 times (see Figure 8.7).

The shape of the triangle not only helps you to see what the likely break-out price would be, but it can also inform you about the trend the market is following. A bearish triangle will have a steeper upper angle (see Figure 8.8), signalling that the market will likely break south before a certain point in time, while a bullish one will have the opposite (see Figure 8.9).

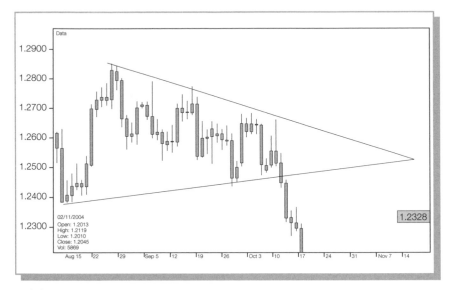

Source: www.babypips.com

Figure 8.7   Example of a symmetrical triangle

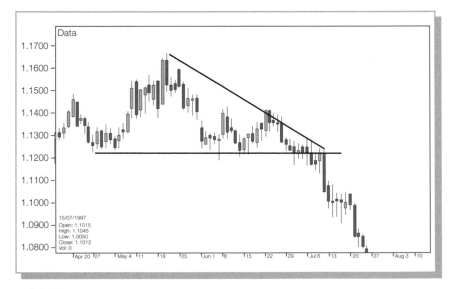

Source: www.babypips.com

Figure 8.8   Example of a down-trending triangle

Source: www.babypips.com

Figure 8.9   Example of an up-trending triangle

The theories behind technical analysis

Behind many of the more widely used forms of technical analysis lie mathematical theories that inform many of the ratios employed in charting programs. Luckily, in this day and age computers can do 99 per cent of the number crunching for you. But a great deal of the analysis discussed above is powered by mathematical assumptions pioneered by a number of 20th-century market theorists.

Dow Theory

Named after Charles Dow, the creator of the Dow Jones Industrial Index, Dow Theory is one of the earliest forms of technical analysis. Dow Theory has come back into vogue recently, but over the last century plus it has swung in and out of fashion with technical analysts. On occasion, it has been used to accurately call the market to uncanny effect (for example, by William P. Hamilton, editor of *The Wall Street Journal*, a matter of days before the Wall Street Crash in 1929). It is not infallible, however.

The core arguments of Dow Theory are as follows:

1 Most of the information driving the market is in the price. Something especially unusual and unanticipated would need to come out of the blue in order for the price to be affected otherwise (a central bank intervention, for example).

2 Markets are driven by three trends: a primary trend which exists so long as the market continues to be able to reach higher peaks; a secondary trend of corrections, lasting between three weeks and three months; and a third trend of small corrections or ripples in the market. Obviously, it was to the primary trend that the likes of Dow and Hamilton paid the most attention.

3 Dow saw bull and bear markets occurring in three phases:

Bull market phases

- Early stage: adventurous buyers come into the market seeking bargains; the best point in the bull market for canny traders to enter the market.

- Middle stage: the bear market matures and more buyers pile into the market. This is when the price covers most of its upwards ground.

- Late phase: the market is now starting to top out as latecomers buy in.

Bear market phases

- Early stage: at the top of the market, volume in trading is still high, but the market has lost its momentum.

- Middle stage: the news flow turns negative and investors begin to sell. The price falls more often than it climbs.

- Later stage: despite false corrections, the market is unable to meet previous highs. More investors are leaving. The news flow has turned distinctly negative. Volume is now low and the price is being driven by sellers.

4 *Lines*: bull markets in particular can conform to a horizontal trajectory for a while, but will then break out sharply upwards. They will tend to trade within narrow bands of around 5 per cent of the price while in this phase. It is less prevalent in bear markets, as optimism is draining out of the market.

5 *Averages*: Dow always used a secondary indicator to confirm trends. In his day, there were two established stock market indexes in the US, the Industrials and the Railroads (partly because railway stocks composed such a big chunk of the listed market in the US circa 1900). He always looked at both indexes before he made a prediction, seeking confirmation of a trend from both before calling the market.

6 *Trends*: Dow looked for trends in the market, just as many traders and technical analysts do today. He was alive to possible reversals occurring as a market failed to beat previous highs and then produced some significant drops below the points established by previous reversals.

7 *Volume*: Dow was one of the first technical analysts to look at volume in the market. This could confirm whether the price was being driven by a lot of investors and traders or only a handful. If the market is dropping and the volume is high, with plenty of trading going on and currency changing hands, then you know this bearish move is a big one. If volume is light and the price is moving, it may just be a false movement and not a significant trend.

Elliott Wave Theory

Ralph Nelson Elliott was an accountant who was forced to retire due to illness in the 1930s and began studying the stock market. He was a keen mathematician, and also familiar with Dow Theory (above). He argued that there were some fundamental mathematical principles behind everything in the universe, promoting natural patterns in physics, biology, astronomy and markets.

In the case of markets, he and his disciples have argued that bull markets move in five distinct waves – three upward trends (impulse trends) interrupted by two corrections (corrective waves). This in turn is followed by two downward trends, interrupted by a single bullish correction.

Elliott Waves need to be taken with a pinch of salt, as they don't stand up to rigorous scientific scrutiny. Some analysts argue they apply only when there is solid underlying economic growth (i.e. the global economy is powering ahead and not limping along as it was at the time of writing).

Underlying Elliott Wave Theory are Fibonacci numbers. Fibonacci was a medieval Italian mathematician, who created a number series based on adding together the two previous numbers (1, 1, 2, 3, 5, 8, 13, etc.). A ratio can be created by dividing one Fibonacci number by the one in front:

$2/3 = 0.67$
$3/5 = 0.6$
$5/8 = 0.625$
$8/13 = 0.615$
$13/21 = 0.619$

If you start dividing each number by the previous one, again after the first few numbers, you end up with:

$13/8 = 1.625$
$21/13 = 1.615$
$34/21 = 1.619$

And so on. The importance of this seemingly irrelevant exercise in mathematics is that Elliott Waves are meant to conform to Fibonacci ratios. Technical analysts will use these ratios to work out what price objectives will be in advance.

Let's go back to the original sequence of waves in the bull market. Remember, Elliott claimed the bull market, regardless of the time-scale being used, would break down into five distinct phases or waves, three up and two down, before running out of steam. Let's assume you think a bull market is developing and you want to use Elliott Wave Theory. You would take the top of the first 'peak' in your proposed bull, multiply it by the magic number 1.618, and add it to the bottom of the first 'trough' (i.e. the end of the first corrective wave). The theory goes that this should give you an indicator of where the peak of the next impulse trend will be. To find the ultimate peak in the market, you would then take the height of the first wave, multiply it by 3.236 (1.618 × 2) and add it to the trough established by the first corrective wave. A basic pattern is shown in Figure 8.10.

In essence, the bull market is meant to conform to a 5:3:5:3:5 ratio sequence, while the bear will follow a 5:3:5 correction (although sometimes it will pursue what is known as a 'flat correction' of 3:3:5).

You will sometimes hear analysts talking about 'Fibonacci retracements'. This means they are applying lines to the chart based on these

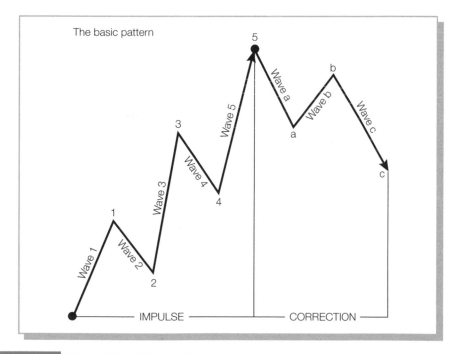

Figure 8.10   Basic Elliott Wave pattern

ratios and that they expect them to provide some kind of resistance level to the current move in the market. The usual ratios are: 61.8 per cent, 38.2 per cent and a more prosaic 50 per cent. Each can be used to project a potential resistance level, whether the analyst is looking for a possible peak to a market (and therefore a price objective, a point where he may want to exit), or a point where a bear market is likely to correct and move upwards.

Gann Theory

William Delbert Gann was a cotton trader who made his name as a predictor of movements in commodities and share prices in the first three decades of the 20th century. He has become something of a legendary figure in chartist circles, partly because he was so successful, but also because he claimed many of his ideas were formed by his studies of ancient mathematics and geometry, including the designs of temples in India and Egypt.

Gann looked for mathematical, recurring patterns in nature and in astronomy, and based many of his ideas on the relationship between time and space. He famously predicted the price of a bag of wheat on 30 September 1909 would be $1.20, even though the market that day was still only around $1.09 an hour before the close. It rose to close at $1.20. The fact that Gann was being shadowed by a journalist at the time helped to reinforce his fame on Wall Street.

Gann was notoriously secretive about his methods, but some of what he used has leaked out over time (Gann died in 1955). For example, Gann angles are lines on a chart that are meant to help predict future turning points in the market. Gann argued that the price range from a significant low point to a high point is divisible by eight. A line can be drawn mid-way between these – the 4/8 line – which can provide a good indicator of possible support or resistance levels. The $^5/_8$ level is considered the next strongest level.

Gann theories are often expressed as 'fan' lines – a series of diagonal lines on a chart that the technical analyst will use to provide him with a predictive edge. The 4/8 line can be drawn at exactly 45 degrees, while the next most significant fan lines can be drawn at 63.75 degrees and 26.25 degrees.

Gann used other astrological theories to predict natural and political events. Here he crossed the line from what I would call scientific calculation into astrology. Some traders buy into this, others don't. Much will depend on how much weight you as an individual place on astrology. Suffice to say, Gann felt that financial markets were subject to the same universal laws of numbers as everything else. His results certainly indicate he was on to something.

Summary

Technical analysis is used by traders in the forex market to try to make sense of numbers and of the market psychology driving those numbers. Analysts want to bring order to the sometimes chaotic jumble of lines and numbers that represents the various financial markets on a trading screen. They want to look for patterns they can act on. In this chapter I have really only scratched the surface of what can be an intriguing and in-depth topic.

There is already a considerable body of literature on technical analysis available for consultation, both online and in print (Chapter 9 contains some of the more significant works).

Much of the above analysis and calculation can, thankfully, be performed at a touch of a button; the charting facilities that exist on most sophisticated forex trading platforms will be able to produce most of the basic technical analysis you might want. This chapter should help you to begin to understand what some market analysts and chartists are talking about, but it is not essential to becoming a successful trader. Indeed, there are some traders who have been able to build perfectly good trading systems and go on to make a lot of money without any technical analysis whatsoever.

Technical analysis is a subject that those of a mathematical bent can find themselves becoming completely immersed in; it can be fun, but it can also be possible to over-analyse a market and never actually place any trades – or make any money. Perhaps the best way to start down this road is to use a few indicators in the course of your early trading and see what works for you.

9

Further resources for the forex trader

The range of resources available to the novice FX trader is enormous. In terms of the support available and the amount of additional information online, the new trader is better placed than ever before. Filtering out what you really need, and what will actually add value to your trading strategy, is the real task. Trial and error will help you find the resources that really lend themselves to what you are setting out to achieve with your spread betting accounts.

From the brokerages

As a client of a forex brokerage, you may have at your fingertips a really quite wonderful range of resources, some of which is now integral to the various trading platforms. Depending on who you trade with, this may now include the following:

- Live news and economic announcements are available via the newswires, something which costs professional traders thousands of pounds to have delivered to them on their desktops. News can be delayed by 15 minutes (much of the free news published by newswires on the internet has a 15-minute delay, as the real premium is having this information as it goes out, literally in less than a second). Having said that, the big newswires are now beginning to allow some brokers to broadcast their information on a live basis on their trading platforms.

- Additional technical analysis is now being liberally disseminated by in-house teams of analysts via email and YouTube. For example, Saxo Bank currently offers excellent daily forex coverage and analysis. Many traders will have a favourite analyst or team of analysts they will follow. This includes some of the analysts at the big investment banks.

- Brokerages also offer their customers free seminars. These can be live and in person, or via a webinar. They continue to invest money in making sure new customers are being properly educated, but in addition they host some fairly advanced trading seminars as well. The best thing is: they're FREE. If you're a customer and can get to one, it is worth going along as you can also meet other traders and compare notes.

Trading platforms

Not all brokers offer trading platforms and not all traders want to use them. Consequently, some traders buy an off-the-shelf platform for forex trading. This will require extra work installing it and you may also need to buy price feeds independently. To date I have used only proprietary trading platforms, but I have heard that the work involved in setting up your own can be quite laborious and even costly.

The market leader at the time of writing is MetaTrader, which is free to use and easy to integrate to many of the FX brokers' price feeds and trading functionality. You will also find that most of the expert adviser programs written for forex markets have been designed for use with MetaTrader. It is also available for use on mobile phones and PDAs.

Another popular platform is NinjaTrader. Apart from letting you manage your trading book, it has some great analytical features, such as the ability to run historical tests and run back-testing studies of your past trading performance and those of any trading programs you use. It can also be used with more than 300 third-party add-ons and applications written specifically for NinjaTrader.

Charting and technical analysis

If you're interested in charting and technical analysis, it is worth going to www.dailyfx.com. This is a sophisticated site covering the broad gamut of technical analysis, with specific focus on forex. Apart from the ability to do all your charting online with a massive range of indicators, the site runs news and analysis on FX markets and has some great videos from the DailyFX staff of technical analysts. Unfortunately some features are not available to residents of the United States.

Trading signals

These are services run by analysts who will monitor the FX markets and email you trading signals, often with commentary attached explaining why they are recommending a particular trade. It is up to you whether you decide to go with it or not. Some are entirely free, and some combine free with premium content. A couple of examples include the following:

Financial Trend Analysis (www.ftanalysis.com) – publishes daily signals on 24 currency pairs. Subscribers can receive this as an email every morning. Most of its recommendations are short-term trades in the 3–5-day time frame. It focuses on low-risk, high-return trades with tight stops. It can also provide information on likely support and resistance levels.

First4Trading (www.first4trading.com) – produces forex research for both institutions and individuals. It aims to deliver trading signals for when the main European forex markets wake up at around 07.00, with many trades designed to be closed out before either 13.00 or 16.00. Trades are updated during the day, with updates posted on the website.

Magazines and newspapers

Financial Times (www.ft.com)

I tend to make use of the *FT*'s website rather than the newspaper because it now boasts a great markets section, with many blogs from experienced *FT* journalists and other commentators. The *FT* is a great way to start the day, and I usually like to catch up on overnight news first thing in the morning. Regular features like 'The Short View' are useful for helping to build an idea of the big picture and what the market is thinking.

FXStreet (www.FXstreet.com)

A mine of news, analysis and information for the beginning FX trader. FXStreet is a great one-stop shop if you want to explore many of the available online resources for the trader. It includes technical analysis and charting facilities, an economic calendar, webinars, a learning centre and a huge directory of services. If you bookmark only one FX website, this probably ought to be it.

Safehaven (www.safehaven.com)

This is a great online resource for those interested in the sort of macroeconomic movements that can establish medium- to long-term FX trends. Safehaven has quite a few seasoned authors working for it who produce an impressive volume of market analysis. Worth a read if you are intent on preserving your capital.

Your Trading Edge (www.ytemagazine.com)

Your Trading Edge or YTE is an excellent bi-monthly magazine published in Australia. Although it does not cover FX trading exclusively, and is aimed primarily at traders in Australia, it has broadened its coverage of global financial markets considerably. It is highly technical in nature, so if you favour charting, you will like it. Australian traders tend to be fairly savvy about commodities, too, hence there is plenty of discussion on global commodities markets. If anything can get you trading the Australian dollar, YTE will.

Websites

Twitter (www.twitter.com)

Twitter is increasingly being used by traders as a source of breaking news. This is partly because many journalists and analysts now 'tweet' on a regular basis – sometimes as often as every 30 minutes when the market is open – and partly because it allows you, the trader, to build your own news feed by following the tweeters who interest you.

I've been particularly impressed over the past 18 months by the level of knowledge demonstrated by some of the active tweeters on the market. You can now use software that will help you to collate and monitor your favourite tweeters. By doing this, you are able to build up your own, comprehensive, tailored newsfeed. And it's all free!

YouTube (www.youtube.com)

YouTube is a mine of information on trading, including forex trading. There are new videos being uploaded all the time. It is a reservoir of useful educational material for all levels of trading expertise. Many analysts also use it to broadcast daily commentary.

The Armchair Trader (www.thearmchairtrader.com)

The Armchair Trader has been launched to provide information on margins and spreads for both the spread betting and CFD trading fraternity. It aims to offer an up-to-date picture of the various accounts on the market and the spreads being offered on the most popular markets. In addition, it has news and articles on spread betting and CFD trading. It covers all the markets available via online trading, but I understand plans are afoot to add a dedicated margined FX section in 2012.

Baby Pips (www.babypips.com)

Baby Pips describes itself as an online forex trading school, and it is certainly worth checking out if you are new to forex trading. It goes further than that, however. It includes Baby Pips' Forexpedia, a guide to everything important for forex markets, from central banks to chart patterns, currency codes to trading styles. The best bit about Baby Pips is that it is written very much with the newcomer or intermediate trader in mind and is not in the least bit intimidating. It also has a very useful app for the iPad.

Ashraf Laidi (www.ashraflaidi.com)

Former CMC Markets analyst Ashraf Laidi has his own website and you can also follow him on Twitter. He frequently appears on CNBC and Al Jazeera discussing global forex markets and is one of *FX Week's* top-rated Europe-based FX analysts. Much of Ashraf's output is free.

He has a great interactive economic calendar on his website which allows you to filter out all the economic announcements you don't require. Worth a regular visit.

Television

CNBC and Bloomberg Television are both available via cable networks in the UK and are excellent sources of information on global markets. After lunchtime, their bias tends towards the US markets, with regular updates from the European news teams. If you have a tendency to be up in the middle of the night, you can also get a blow by blow account of what Asian markets are up to.

Both channels offer solid coverage of the currency and commodities markets. I followed them closely during the 2008 financial crisis, and when working for CMC Markets, where TV screens were strategically positioned at every corner of the dealing floor. Some traders like having the TV on in the background all day long, others don't. It can be possible to be caught up in the hysteria of what is going on if you listen too closely, and that can mess with your discipline.

Trading coaches

There is big business in advising and coaching traders, both professional and amateur. Many successful traders have a lucrative side line in training and advising other traders. Some spread bettors like to have someone on the end of the phone they can talk to when they are consistently losing money, who can advise them on where they are perhaps going wrong.

Trading coaches are there to advise on strategy and technique. Some are only a step away from being psychiatrists. They are not investment advisers. They can't tell you whether a trade is a good one or not. They are most useful as an extra pair of eyes, looking over your shoulder – metaphorically or literally – and telling you where you're going wrong.

Trading can be a solitary existence, and having someone you can talk to objectively about your trading can be very helpful indeed for keeping your mind in the right place and helping you to build a winning strategy.

Trading coaches don't come cheap: many of them are consulted by some of the best traders in the City, and some are very experienced in their own right. Retaining one can be expensive, but then again, like a good accountant, they can often save you more money than you pay them.

Trading coaches are best consulted when you are in the doldrums and are taking some fairly consistent losses. It may just be the market, but it may have something to do with the way you are trading.

When choosing a trading coach, make sure they know what they're doing and have a track record in trading and advising successful trading. Word of mouth from other traders is often as good a means as any of finding the right one for you. But be prepared to pay for good advice.

Systematic trading programs/expert advisers

There is a large industry in the US selling software packages that help you to trade by generating buy and sell signals. These are sometimes described as 'black box' trading strategies, expert advisers or trading 'robots'. Over the years, many traders and programmers have designed their own systems for trading, and some of these are now becoming commercially available as software packages.

In the world of hedge funds and investment banking, computer programs are being widely used because computers enjoy a number of advantages over human traders:

1 Computers don't get emotional about losing trades.

2 Computers learn more quickly from their mistakes.

3 Computers can process far more market information, more accurately, than humans can.

4 At the institutional level, computers can trade more quickly than humans and react to price changes in the market more effectively.

Using a computer program to trade for yourself is a hit-and-miss affair. A program will need to be one suited to the particular market you want to trade and the risk parameters you want to use. Using a program that was designed to trade shares to trade forex markets can go badly awry. You will also frequently need to provide it with the historical data it requires to make its calculations, as well as make sure it is hooked up to a current data feed. This in itself can be expensive – live data feeds do not come cheap.

The new generation of trading programs coming onto the market is more flexible and allows you to tailor the programs a little to your own requirements. You are still drawing on the core algorithm for your principal trading signals, but you can adjust it to suit your personal objectives and risk tolerance.

Computer-based trading programs are something of a leap of faith if you have not designed them yourself. Having said that, they must be doing something right because some spread betting companies have been known to close the accounts of traders whom they suspect are using a program-based approach.

Designing your own program to trade can be challenging, unless you are something of a software engineer yourself. It is not a fire-and-forget process: programs need to be constantly updated and tweaked. In addition, they rely heavily on past performance data to inform their trading decisions. What they don't tend to take into consideration is that markets are always changing, they are never static, and this makes them unpredictable.

Reading list

There is a wide and comprehensive range of books available on forex trading, many written by industry insiders or those with professional trading experience. Below are some of those which might help the newcomer with additional insights into the markets and trading in general. Much really depends on which areas of the wide world of financial markets you wish to focus on, and how your trading strategy evolves.

Spread betting

Jones, David (2010) *Spread Betting the Forex Market,* London: Harriman House.

Pryor, Malcolm (2007) *The Financial Spread Betting Handbook,* London: Harriman House.

CFDs

Temple, Peter (2009) *CFDs Made Simple*, London: Harriman House.

Trading

Faith, Curtis M. (2007) *Way of the Turtle,* New York: McGraw-Hill.

Laidi, Ashraf (2008) *Currency Trading and Intermarket Analysis*, London: John Wiley & Sons.

Schwager, Jack (1992) *The New Market Wizards,* New York: Collins Business.

Tharp, Van K. (1998) *Trade Your Way to Financial Freedom,* New York: McGraw-Hill.

Technical analysis

Gann, W.D. (2010) *How to Make Profits Trading in Commodities,* Connecticut: Martino Publishing.

Gifford, Elli (1995) *Technical Analysis – Predicting Price Action in the Market,* London: FT Pitman Publishing.

Murphy, John J. (1998) *Technical Analysis of the Financial Markets*, New York: New York Institute of Finance.

Nison, Steven (2001) *Japanese Candlestick Charts*, London: FT Prentice Hall.

Quantitative finance and trading systems

Chan, Ernest P. (2008) *Quantitative Trading – How to Build Your Own Algorithmic Trading Business*, New York: John Wiley & Sons.

Jaekle, Urban and Tomasini, Emilio (2009) *Trading Systems: A New Approach to Systems Development and Portfolio Optimisation*, London: Harriman House.

10

Careers in FX trading

Some readers may be looking at forex trading as a potential career, rather than as an after-hours activity that can make them more money. I have been writing about and working in the financial industry for 18 years, and during that time I have been witness to remarkable changes in the way money is managed, and also in the way the industry recruits.

In the early 1990s the financial industry was still very male-dominated, and the skills prized were not the skills many employers look for today. There are many more women working in financial services and the world of trading than ever before, and there are even some all-girl trading teams that are making a success of it away from their male peers.

If you are specifically interested in a career in FX trading, this chapter contains some home truths you will need to consider.

The changing world of trading

The world of trading may have changed, but some things have stayed the same. To get started in trading you will generally need to be young: there are some traders still over 40, but most have graduated to other roles within operations, sales, marketing or management. Most of those employed as traders on a full-time basis that I have met are typically under 40. Firms will tend to look to recruit trainees in their 20s.

Degrees are not obligatory. If you are bright, prepared to work hard, and possibly speak one or more foreign languages and have an A-level in Mathematics under your belt, you will likely find someone prepared to give you an interview. What counts is how well you do after that. Elsewhere in this book I discuss the debate about whether good traders are born or made, and the famous 'Turtles' experiment. From my experience, I think it is possible to take someone off the street and make them a good trader, but there needs to be a degree of raw material there. Many extremely bright people have failed – badly –

at trading. But employers often won't know how well a trainee will perform until they have spent some weeks or months on a trading floor.

Investment banks

Most people consider a role with an investment bank if they are interested in trading, and indeed these have been the proving ground of many successful careers over the years. Investment banks such as Goldman Sachs, Merrill Lynch, Morgan Stanley and UBS still act almost as 'trading universities' – there are few successful hedge fund managers who have not done their time working in an investment bank at some point.

Be warned, however. Competition for graduate trainee jobs in investment banks around the world is fierce: candidates are attracted by the prospect of making large amounts of money in a short space of time, and indeed there are few jobs that are better paid. Because of this, investment banks can take their pick of potential candidates. Trainee traders work very long hours and have little social life to speak of. Lurid newspaper stories of investment bankers regularly spending their evenings in saucy nightclubs are overblown: they are usually the ones buying take-out coffee at seven o'clock in the evening because they've got a couple of hours still to go. They are also the ones who look at you blankly when you talk about the rush hour: they travel in before anyone else and they go home long after everyone else.

Still, investment banks are important conduits in the whole interbank FX market. Even three to five years in an investment bank can pave the way to a successful career in forex, and if you've lucky you may well be able to retire by the age of 45.

The world is changing, however. The march of regulation is catching up with investment banks, and they are being forced to divest themselves of their proprietary ('prop') trading divisions. This will mean fewer opportunities on trading floors going forward. Many prop traders are now seeking roles in the world of hedge funds, but this can be even more demanding without the cushion of a large institution around you. Others are spinning out their prop trading operations into separate businesses and retaining some level of strategic interest. But those who are staying on to trade at investment banks are going to have less independence and will be prized more for their sales skills than their knowledge of how markets behave.

Hedge funds

Hedge funds employ a lot of traders, to be sure, but FX funds are a special breed unto themselves. Most dedicated FX funds are entirely systematic. This means the vast bulk of their trades are informed by sophisticated computer programs. The role of FX fund manager has really wandered out of the realm of trading and into that of computer science. Big FX funds will tend to be looking for bright post-graduates with degrees in Mathematics, Physics and computer-related studies. Some of them will only really look at candidates with some form of related PhD thesis under their belts. Emphasis seems to be less on knowledge of the financial markets and more on how academic disciplines can be applied to money management.

Outside specialist FX funds, there is an element of forex activity in the global macro strategy. These are big funds which have the mandate to take bets in just about any market that looks interesting, be it equities, bonds, commodities, interest rates or forex. They still employ trading teams, but even the biggest won't have a huge trading floor like a big bank will. There are no macro funds in Canary Wharf to my knowledge. Forex is an element of the global macro strategy, but only part of it.

Traders working in a hedge fund will generally be reporting to the portfolio manager. It is really the fund's manager who is making all the investment decisions. The traders are there to execute them, ideally at the best price and when the time is right. They will also need to provide the manager with feedback and updates on what the portfolio is doing. With a big FX fund, someone still needs to keep tabs on the trades the computer is signalling in the market. But go into the trading room of a big hedge fund and you'll be struck at how quiet it can be.

Hedge funds tend to hire their traders from somewhere else: they're not in the business of taking on and training graduates. Traders at big hedge funds can graduate onto the roles with more responsibility if they do well, but to get there they will need a track record with another institution (e.g. an investment bank). Frequently a prop trader will leave a bank and take a number of their colleagues with them to start a fund. As it grows, they will tap other colleagues for roles in the organisation. It pays to stay networked.

Sales trading

Sales trading roles exist in a number of organisations. Sales traders are there to take the orders from clients and get them the best price in the market. In many firms this is not an advisory role: you are not even allowed to give the client advice, other than on timing and liquidity (e.g. letting them know what the GBP/USD market is looking like, or how quickly you estimate it will take to place a large trade). Sales traders seem to spend a lot of time on the phone to clients or staring vacantly at their screens.

Many different firms will recruit sales traders; however, unless the firm is an FX specialist, you will probably be executing trades across a wide range of markets, particularly equities, where the sales trading function is more valued. Solid client relationships are an important part of the sales trader's value to a firm, and if he changes job it is often expected that he will bring business with him. It requires excellent interpersonal skills and ideally more than one language.

Spread betting, CFD and forex firms

The retail trading industry is continuing to grow, with more firms springing up all the time. These will recruit traders to help clients place trades over the phone, as well as to consistently hedge market risk. Although the number of firms and the volumes of trading are increasing, so is the level of automation in online retail trading. Fewer clients feel the need to place telephone trades, so much of the emphasis at the larger firms seems to be shifting to risk management – making sure the firm is hedged against any large client positions. It is more of a reactive role, fighting fires rather than making money.

Programming

The real growth area in FX trading is in programming. Large firms of all shapes and sizes continue to invest money in front-end technical development. Off-the-shelf applications are of no use in competitive portfolio management: if everyone uses the same quantitative model, they will all achieve similar results.

This means many banks and funds are in the business of building first-class technology teams intended to develop proprietary internal systems. There is a range of programs that developers will need to be familiar with, while knowledge of financial markets per se is less necessary (read this book cover to cover and you will know more about forex than many developers already working in banks and hedge funds).

Knowledge of Java and C++ seems to be required in many instances.

Wealth management and advisory

Appetite for forex as an investment is growing as wealthy investors realise that they made little, if any, long-term gain from equities in the last decade. The poor performance of share markets in recent years has also caused investors to seek out opportunities in other asset classes. This means traditional money managers, such as private banks and brokers, are having to expand their level of knowledge to include forex. I fully expect that the demand for individuals who can make money for clients in FX markets – as opposed to helping them simply move it cost effectively around the world – will increase going forwards.

Beyond that, there are still many firms offering advisory FX trading. This is where the customer is paying an additional fee for advice from the trader as to which positions to take. Many private FX traders like to be guided by a more experienced head, especially earlier on in their trading career.

Advisory traders are expected to build their own 'book' of business by finding clients prepared to open accounts with their firm. As with the sales trader above, this role requires good interpersonal skills, as well as a head for the markets. Clients will expect results, and there is a high degree of pressure to deliver, as there is with many FX trading jobs.

Trading academies

Firms are always hunting for new trading talent, however, and if you are good, it can lead to a profitable FX trading career. There are several schemes out there, some better than others, designed to help talented traders make money. The better ones will usually require some sort of independently documented track record before they accept you. In return they provide institutional-quality trading facilities, coaching, and the opportunity to manage the money of others as well.

This approach to nurturing FX talent is relatively new. Some of the trading arcades I have visited also place money with some of their consistently solid clients. If you can produce a regular return – it does not have to be stratospheric – across different market environments, you could get noticed. Your broker can usually help in certifying your trading performance to date by allowing access to your records – that way a third party should be able to establish how credible you are.

These 'trader nurseries' are a little bit like the soccer academies supported by some UK Premiership football clubs – they are training players, but they are also seeking new talent they can profit from in the medium term.

Outside the financial industry

It is important to stress here that FX trading is not restricted to the financial industry. Many, many companies incur forex liabilities in the course of conducting international trade, or supporting offices and businesses in many different countries. In addition, foreign currency is needed to make large overseas acquisitions. These businesses by definition need somebody to help them with managing their foreign exchange.

This function can be outsourced to banks for a fee, but larger firms have been known to retain an internal forex management unit, often within their treasury or finance function. Here, the emphasis is on reducing or eliminating foreign currency risks, via the use of hedging or forwards. Frequently, the trader will be dealing with banks directly and reporting to treasury management. I have heard tell that some traders have been recruited directly from accounting staff or have had trading added to other financial responsibilities. Firms also hire experienced traders to manage their foreign currency liabilities if they are doing plenty of overseas trading. Just consider how much forex goes through the accounts of an Apple or a McDonald's.

It may be that, should you already be employed within a firm in a finance capacity, aptitude and interest in FX markets could land you an internal role helping to manage your company's FX book. It can be cheaper than getting a bank to do it for you, plus an internal trader has better day-to-day knowledge of what the company is likely to need and is more easily accessible.

Doing it yourself

Finally, you can simply set up on your own. This is easier in some jurisdictions than others. Many successful money managers have begun life asking friends and family to write them a cheque, and if they prove successful, are able to attract more investment via word of mouth. If you have good connections and can produce results, you can accrue substantial sums.

However, if you are doing this for a fee, be aware that there are regulatory and legal responsibilities you will need to comply with. Most countries these days require investment managers to pass some form of exam and to be regularly inspected to ensure they comply with the standards expected of money managers. This will bring with it substantial costs, but there is no real way around this.

Asia and North America in particular seem to be excellent venues for the DIY approach – by this I mean setting up to make a living out of FX trading, trading for yourself and charging others a fee to make money for them. Much will depend on your ability to attract capital, to grow your business responsibly, and ultimately to generate the performance numbers your clients will want to see. Given that cash rates are so low in most countries at the time of writing, the performance benchmark is not as high as it used to be. Consistency and good risk management are equally important, however.

Glossary of forex trading and other financial market terms

ADX (average directional index) A popular type of technical analysis, used to measure the strength of a trend. On its own it does not indicate whether this is an up or down trend, but an ADX of 20–30 can represent the beginning of a trend. It is often used in conjunction with other data by trend followers.

Aussie Slang term for the Australian dollar (AUD).

Bid price Also known as the 'buy' price. The price used to open a long bet, or to close a short bet.

Bid/offer spread The difference between the buy and the sell price, and one of the ways spread betting companies make their money. Also, wider spreads reflect markets where there is less liquidity.

Binary bet A type of spread bet where you win or lose depending on whether a market price crosses a specific level. Traders either collect 100 per cent of their winnings or get nothing.

Bollinger band A technical analysis term for two lines plotted above and below the moving average. They are meant to help to measure the relative volatility of the market concerned.

Break out When a currency price breaks out of a band within which it has been trading for a period of time.

Cable A term frequently used to describe the GBP/USD currency market.

CFD (contract for difference) A popular over-the-counter trading instrument that is now one of the most widely traded retail derivatives outside the UK and Ireland. Unlike spread bets, however, CFDs do incur tax. They are often used for FX trading.

Counterparty The party on the other side of your trade or investment. It takes two to tango with any financial transaction. In the case of spread betting, this will be your spread betting company, but in turn your spread betting company will have credit lines with banks, as well as open trades with prime brokers.

CPI (Consumer Price Index) A common means of measuring the rate of inflation in an economy, based on a basket of typically purchased goods.

Demo account A trial account offered by many trading companies which you can open with no money. Usually you will be able to spread bet on only a restricted list of markets, and often you will have access to the platform for only a limited period of time – two weeks is typical. The intention is to give you a feel for the functionality of the platform, as well as to allow you to trade – and potentially make mistakes – without risking any real money.

Deposit requirement The amount of money a spread betting company requires the trader to have on deposit in order to place a bet in a given market. This will vary from company to company.

Direct market access (DMA) The process of trading directly on the market, or at the very least being able to see individual orders coming into the market and being able to act on them.

ETF (exchange-traded fund) A fund based on an index, possibly a currency index. It can be bought and sold on a stock exchange, like a share. It charges a small annual fee to the owner.

Eurodollar The market for lending and borrowing US dollars outside the United States' banking system.

Expert adviser A systematic trading program, usually a form of computer program that will seek buy-and-sell signals across dozens of currency pairs. They can usually be bought commercially and can advise the trader when to open and close positions.

The Fed Slang term for the Federal Reserve, the US central bank.

Forward An agreement to buy or sell a currency at a fixed rate at some point in the future. Unlike a futures contract, the price does not fluctuate. There is usually a fee attached to the transaction.

Gapping Sudden change in the price of a market, often caused by extraneous factors. The market often moves too quickly for the retail trader to respond during this period. The price then often stabilises at a new level.

Greenback Slang term used to describe the US dollar.

If done A type of trading order that takes place if a previous order is executed. For example, this can be used to place a stop loss at the same time another order is opened. Some traders use 'if done' orders if they cannot be at the screens all the time and need to take advantage of potential price levels.

Interbank market The market for foreign exchange which exists between banks and other major market participants. This determines the price at which currencies are traded.

Intra-day Something that occurs within a typical trading day: an intra-day trade is one opened and closed within a single trading day.

Japanese candlestick A form of technical analysis pioneered by 16th-century Japanese rice traders. It shows not only the highest and lowest points reached by a market over a given time frame but also the opening and closing price at either end of the time frame. Candlesticks can be defined by the user to cover any regular time period they care to analyse.

JGB (Japanese government bond) Debt issued by the Japanese government. The benchmark price of Japan's sovereign debt is the 10-year JGB.

Leverage A term commonly used to describe the act of borrowing money with which to invest.

LIBOR London Interbank Offered Rate, the daily rate used by banks to borrow from each other in the London money markets. This is frequently used as a benchmark rate for financial products.

Limit order An automatic instruction to the broker to close your bet once a specific price level is reached.

Liquidity A term used to describe how easy it is to buy and sell in a market. A less liquid market can make it harder for someone to buy or sell large quantities of an asset. If markets become less liquid, spreads tend to get wider.

Loonie Slang term used by currency traders to describe the Canadian dollar.

Margin The minimum amount of money you need to commit to open a spread bet. Your broker should allow you to deposit more than this if you need to.

Margin call If you are close to losing your margin amount, your broker may call you up to ask you to deposit more money in the trade. For example, if you staked £100, you might get a call when you had lost £80. Brokers will make margin calls on a discretionary basis.

Moving average A line on a chart generated by using the average price performance over a specific period of previous days. By keeping tabs on the moving average, traders can see how the current market behaviour compares with past performance. Typical moving average series include 200-, 50-, and 30-day periods.

NTR (notional trading requirement) A measurement used by brokers to determine whether you have enough money in your account to fund a trade. This goes beyond stumping up the initial margin. Each market has a different bet size requirement which the company will apply to your cash balance to determine whether you can afford the bet if the market turns against you.

OCO (one cancels the other) A type of spread betting order which will instruct the platform to cancel a second order if a primary order is executed. For example, if an automatic take profit order occurs, the trader will also want to make sure that the stop loss protecting the trade has also been cancelled. This is an automated order which can be added to ensure that something happens even when you are away from your trading screen.

Offer price Also known as the sell price, this is the price used to go short of a market, or to close a long bet.

OTC (over the counter) A trade that is not taking place in an open exchange. Most liquid futures markets (although not all of them) are now based on one of the big derivatives exchanges.

Peg Process by which one currency will trade roughly in line with another. Its central bank will buy and sell currency to try to maintain the peg. It is not always successful.

Physical market A market based on real assets, such as shares. Not a market in futures or other derivative instruments. A CFD account is a derivatives account; a share trading account is a physical assets account.

Pip A term used in foreign exchange trading circles to mean the decimal point furthest to the right on any forex quote. A currency is described as moving a certain number of 'pips'. If, for example, yen dropped from 84.62 against the US dollar to 84.51, it would have dropped 11 pips.

Point A single 'unit' of the market you are spread betting. This will vary from market to market. Many stock market indexes are quoted in points already. This is also the number you are betting on. It is usually the number on the far right of any market quote.

Prop trading Trading carried out by a bank or brokerage for its own account.

Quote currency The second currency quoted as part of a forex pair –

the number to the right of the slash. It is the fluctuations in the price of this currency against the currency on the left that you are trading.

Range bound When a currency is restricted to a trading range determined by resistance and support levels.

Resistance level A level at which a market or price repeatedly drops back.

Rollover The process of automatically renewing a trade overnight or when it reaches its expiry date. This usually incurs a financing charge from the spread betting company.

RPI (Retail Price Index) Similar to the CPI (see above), this is a means of measuring inflation in a particular economy. It does not, however, include housing costs such as mortgage repayments.

RSI (Relative Strength Index) An indicator used to demonstrate whether a market is being overbought or oversold, using historical prices as a reference. Usually, an RSI of more than 70 indicates an overbought market, and one under 30 an oversold one.

Short When you go short on a market, you are in a position to make money if the market is going down in value.

Short sterling A contract that allows the trader to take advantage of changes in UK base rates. Its price is based on future interest rate expectations, and is calculated by subtracting the expected rate from 100.

Spot price The price for settlement of a particular future were it to be settled today. Sometimes this is calculated using sophisticated mathematical estimates. It is not always possible to trade on the spot price, but it is becoming increasingly common in trading circles.

Spread betting A type of trading account available only to residents in the UK and Ireland. Profits are tax free as it is treated as gambling by the local tax authorities.

Stop loss An automatic order to your broker to close your position if it reaches a specified price. It is used to protect traders from major losses.

Support level A point at which a market or price bounces back. It fails repeatedly to pass this level. A support level informs traders' expectations of the behaviour of that price.

Swing trading The practice of repeatedly trading the same market both short and long while it is trading between two ranges. The swing trader actively exploits price drops as well as price rises.

Swissie Slang term for the Swiss franc (CHF).

Systematic trading Trading forex markets using a specific rules-based system, often informed by signals from a computer program. This is a purely quantitative approach to markets.

Technical analysis Using charts and various price indicators to try to predict how a market is likely to behave in the future.

Tick Term used to describe the minimum price unit by which a market can change. In spread betting, this will be the 'points' you stake money against.

Trading the news Approach to FX trading that focuses on fundamental factors such as inflation, trade flows, national debt and interest rates. The trader is looking at the economic situation and relying less on technical indicators.

Trailing stop loss A type of stop loss that trails dynamically behind the trade. You need to decide how far behind it follows. If the market then falls back, it closes the trade. This allows you to lock in profits from a trade even when you are away from your trading screen. Not all brokers offer trailing stop losses, but they are becoming increasingly popular.

Appendix: Brokers comparison

Name	Website	Accounts	Minimum account size	Platform	Further resources	Notes	Email
Alpari	www.alpari.co.uk	FX, CFDs, spread betting	200	Meta Trader 4, Systematic, demo account	Education, research, seminars	Large firm with 50 offices globally, no restrictions on scalping or using expert advisers, 500 to 1 leverage on some accounts	info@alpari.co.uk
CMC Markets	cmcmarkets.com	FX, CFDs, spread betting	100	Proprietary trading platforms, available via mobile, tablet and Internet, demo account	Education, research, seminars	Customisable margin and portfolio mixer on CFD accounts, mobile and tablet platforms, lengthy track record in FX broking	info@cmcmarkets.co.uk
eToro	www.etoro.com	FX	50	Web Trader, OpenBook, Mobile Trader, demo account	Education, research, seminars, social trading, Islamic accounts	Strong play on using social media to help traders interact	Via internet site

Name	Website	Accounts	Minimum account size	Platform	Further resources	Notes	Email
FXCM	www.fxcm.com	FX, CFDs, spread betting	£50 spread betting, $2,000 FX, $50,000 for Active Trader	Meta Trader 4, Active Trader	Education, research, seminars, online and mobile trading, demo account	Welcomes expert advisers, online and mobile trading, demo accounts	See website
FXPro	www.fxpro.com	FX		Meta Trader 4, ECN	Trade interbank market, online and mobile solutions, demo account	Accounts in five different currencies including CHF, used by professional traders	info@fxpro.co.uk
FX Solutions	www.fxsolutions.com	FX	250	Meta Trader 4, GTS Pro, GTS Web, FX AccuCharts	Demo accounts, training webinars	Over 300 in-house automated trading systems	
IG Markets	www.igmarkets.com	FX, CFDs, spread betting	No minimum	PureDeal, Insight	Demo accounts, education, training seminars, online and mobile trading	One of the largest CFD brokers globally	helpdesk@igmarkets.com

Name	Website	Accounts	Minimum account size	Platform	Further resources	Notes	Email
Internaxx	www.internaxx.lu	FX, CFDs, swaps	10000	Proprietary trading platform	Free-of-charge trading for one month, online trading	Offshore firm based in Luxembourg, part of the TD Waterhouse group	info@internaxx.lu
MIG Bank	www.migbank.com	FX, CFDs	2000	Meta Trader 4	Demo account (30 days), in-house systematic programs, online and mobile trading	Customers can see the order mark-up	info@migbank.com
Saxo Bank	www.saxobank.com	FX, CFDs, futures, options	2000	Saxo Trader	Trademaker platform provides informed trades, Tradementor online video education, mobile trading	Major institutional provider of forex trading, particularly in Europe	See website for regional offices
Vantage FX	www.vantagefx.com	FX	500	Meta Trader 4	Test expert advisers, build strategies using FX Strategy Builder	Australian broker now expanding abroad	accounts@vantagefx.com

Source: www.thearmchairtrader.com

Index